THE IKKŌ-IKKI
ART OF WAR

The Ikkō-ikki go to war, showing their simple armour and the flags bearing the six character and nine character variations of the invocation of the name of Amida Buddha (Detail from Picture 97)

THE IKKŌ-IKKI ART OF WAR

as illustrated in the military chronicles

Stephen Turnbull

For John Cruickshank,
with thanks for many years of inspiration

The cover picture is a detail from a print depicting Komizucha of Negoroji in action against Toyotomi Hideyoshi at Negoroji in 1585

By the same author:

The Samurai Art of War as illustrated in Hōjō Godai ki (2021)

This book is a
JAPAN ARCHIVE
publication.

For more information please visit

www.stephenturnbull.com

ISBN-9798796811474

CONTENTS

The defence of the Ishiyama Honganji using firearms. The Ikkō-ikki were early users of the European harquebus on a large scale, an innovation customarily associated with their greatest enemy Oda Nobunaga (Detail from Picture 59)

INTRODUCTION

Who were the Ikkō-ikki?

The conflicts that engulfed Japan during the Sengoku Period — the country's so-called "Age of War" that is roughly coterminous with the sixteenth century — involved many types of warriors in addition to the élite samurai who owed loyalty to their own daimyo (warlord). This was because the hierarchical model on which the samurai depended was only one of two possibilities for contemporary governance that had arisen out of the breakdown of central authority following the Ōnin War of 1467-77. The other pattern was for local *kokujin* (provincial men) and *jizamurai* (local samurai/farmers) to form an ikki (confederacy or league) when danger threatened. An ikki was a voluntary armed organisation run ideally on egalitarian lines, and among those groups whose allegiance took this form were the Ikkō-ikki: the "Single-minded League", whose Buddhist faith provided the "glue" that held them together.

The *monto* (followers or disciples) of the Ikkō-ikki belonged specifically to one branch of Jōdo-Shinshū (The True Pure Land Sect), that went under the name of the Honganji (The Temple of the Original Vow). Other militant Buddhist ikki existed who had a similar faith which they held in common, but over the centuries the Ikkō-ikki have become the best known of all Japan's sectarian warriors. Sustained by their passionate belief in the salvation guaranteed by Amida Buddha, the fanatical Ikkō-ikki *monto* welcomed fighting because their faith promised that paradise was the immediate reward for death in battle, and nothing daunted them.

The majority of the *monto* were part-time warriors, but many of their leaders were modestly wealthy men of samurai rank, for whom the European terms "barons" or "gentry" provide useful analogies. Their religious beliefs and a fierce independence were the elements they held most in common and, when it came to making war, they proved the equal of more secular opponents. This dramatic situation was illustrated most vividly by the Ikkō-ikki's ten year-long armed opposition to the rise to power of Japan's first unifier: Oda Nobunaga (1534-82). The events of that war make up the core of this book.

The Ikkō-ikki's leader at the time of Nobunaga was the Shinshū priest Kennyo Kōsa (1543-92), who led and inspired his fellow devotees from their fortified "cathedral" of Ishiyama Honganji, an almost impregnable defensive structure built where Osaka castle now stands. The so-called Ishiyama War was conducted intermittently between 1570 and 1580 and made up overall the longest siege in the whole of Japanese history.

Two important points must be made at this stage regarding the make-up of the Ikkō-ikki armies. First, it is highly misleading to refer to them as "warrior monks", because their organisation attracted samurai, farmers and townsmen in rural communities of shared religious beliefs, not within monasteries. In fact the teachings of Shinran (1173-1262) with whom the sect originated, had revolutionised Japanese Buddhism by doing away with the duality of monasticism and laity and replacing it with a new emphasis on spiritual egalitarianism. A good European analogy to the Ikkō-ikki would be the Hussites of fifteenth century Bohemia or the extreme Puritan communities that arose a century later during the Reformation. Linked by zeal for their beliefs under the leadership of charismatic preachers, they formed self-governing communities defended by armies. So it was with the Ikkō-ikki, although several coteries of genuine "warrior monks" did exist elsewhere during the Sengoku Period in the form of the *sōhei* (priest soldiers) who fought besides and sometimes against the Ikkō-ikki. In the pages which follow we will note in particular the Tendai sect warrior monks of the Enryakuji on Mount Hiei to the north-east of Kyoto and the militant Shingon sect adherents of Negoroji in Kii province.

The second point to note is that not all ikki were religious, and not all religious ikki were Ikko-ikki. There was also great rivalry between the ikki from different Buddhist sects, a factor which Oda Nobunaga exploited on many occasions. Considerable enmity also existed within Jōdo-Shinshū itself, whose other branches objected to the primacy assumed and exerted so vigorously by the aggressive Honganji faction. This too would be manipulated by their rivals.

All in all, however, the Ikko-ikki dominate the narrative of sectarian militarism until the surrender of the Ishiyama Honganji in 1580. Under Nobunaga's successor Toyotomi Hideyoshi (1537-98) militant religious opposition continued in a different form from the monks of Negoroji who had once helped Nobunaga. In 1584 they allied themselves to Hideyoshi's rival Tokugawa Ieyasu (1542-1616), and Hideyoshi's subsequent campaign against them and the Saika-ikki, to which a later section of this book is dedicated, would represent the last gasp of militant Buddhist resistance to the unification of Japan.

This book presents in a pictorial form the events leading up to and including the Ishiyama War of 1570 to 1580 and then takes the story forward through Hideyoshi's wars to the division of the Honganji into two rival yet peaceful organisations in 1602. It includes much original information about the appearance, the armaments and the remarkable military achievements of the dauntless Ikkō-ikki *monto* who fought as fiercely and skilfully as any of their supposedly superior samurai opponents.

The most important foe of the Honganji was always Oda Nobunaga. Throughout this time the continued existence of and resistance by the Ikkō-ikki served at the very least to provide a nagging background noise to Nobunaga's personal ambitions to rule Japan, but when active hostilities were conducted against him by the *monto* the fighting was as fierce as anything that Nobunaga encountered from his more secular foes. From Ishiyama Honganji, from other Ikkō-ikki branches in places like the Nagashima Delta and the mountains of Kaga Province — (and from other sectarian ikki) — came devoted and highly trained armies who were early innovators in the new military technology of European-style firearms, an accomplishment that Nobunaga experienced at first hand in 1576 when a bullet fired from a Honganji harquebus wounded him in the leg.

In the companion volume to this work: *The Samurai Art of War as illustrated in Hōjō Godai ki* (published in 2021), I carried out a similar exercise to this one by presenting a pictorial history of the Hōjō clan of Odawara as revealed in the 1659 illustrated version of the Hōjō's own epic chronicle. In that book I was able to include all ninety pictures from the original work. This book is slightly different. It draws instead on four woodblock printed books published within a space of eighty years during the nineteenth century. Each is a classic *ehon* (illustrated book) version of a *gunkimono* (war tale): an elaborate retelling of historical events. Taken together, the works cover the history of the Ishiyama War in a comprehensive fashion alongside Oda Nobunaga's other military campaigns. Most of the episodes described in the *ehon* are illustrated, out of which I have selected for this volume 101 images that are of particular relevance to the Ishiyama War and the brave Ikkō-ikki who fought in the conflict for so long.

The first of my two main sources is entitled *Ehon Shūi Shinchō ki* (The illustrated book of gleanings from the chronicle of Nobunaga: referred to henceforward as ESSK) which was published in 1803 with pictures by two artists called Niwa Tōkei (1760-1822) and Ryūkōsai Nyokei (dates unknown). Its twenty-three volumes cover the events of the Ishiyama War to a background of Nobunaga's reign and that of his successors. The second: *Ehon Ishiyama Kassen Gunki* (The illustrated book of the war tale of the Ishiyama War: EIKG) was published in 1881 and is an outstanding example of the late flowering of the woodblock printer's art. The illustrator was Matsukawa Hanzan, and the thirty-volume work covers the time from the foundation of Ishiyama Honganji to its division into two branches early in the seventeenth century. Finally, I have included a handful of illustrations from two other books that cover topics neglected in the above works. These are Okada Gyokuzan's well-known *Ehon Taikō ki* (The illustrated chronicle of the Taikō; [i.e. Toyotomi Hideyoshi]: ETK) of 1799 and *Ehon Toyotomi kunkō ki* (Illustrated chronicle of the meritorious deeds of Toyotomi [Hideyoshi]: ETKK) of 1855 by the famous artist Kuniyoshi. In the pages which follow the locations of the pictures in the original sources are identified in the form "EIKG 1,12": i.e. "Part 1, Vol. 12".

Unlike the pictures in the 1659 *Hōjō Godai ki*, each of which is a single page illustration, the images in these works (apart from a handful of single-subject portraits) are double-page spreads which are presented in the original books as two separate representations set within individual frames. For this work I have spliced the pairs of illustrations electronically to make them into one picture to allow the reader to see the drawings as they would have been produced by the original artists.

Just as was the case with the pictures of the Hōjō from the seventeenth century, the illustrations assembled here from two hundred years later represent an important stage in the development of an image; not in this case of the samurai warrior, but of the Ikkō-ikki as an organisation and the individuals who belonged to it. As a recent study has shown, this was a time when the concept of a ten year-long "Ishiyama War" and the centrality to it of the Honganji's Ikkō-ikki were taking shape.[1] In these heroic illustrations the *monto* are presented as plucky lower class fellows who fought greater powers while being sustained by their fervent faith.

In the pages which follow these remarkable illustrations of a unique and often neglected military culture are presented in a published work for the first time in a century and a half. They show fighting of course, including sieges and naval battles, and weapons ranging from ancient *naginata* (glaives) to contemporary firearms are depicted in detail, but these topics are presented to a background of the sincere religious devotion that characterised the military life of the Ikkō-ikki. So we see (and can almost hear!) the chanting of the *nenbutsu* (the invocation of Amida Buddha) as the *monto* go to war at the urging of their priests. Prayers are flung across the moats of castles as if they were bullets; a holy light issues from opened scrolls and ghostly apparitions of terrifying saintly men hover above a noble victim felled by the sword of a Buddhist warrior. This was the Art of War of the Ikkō-ikki of Ishiyama Honganji who went into battle in a dramatic act of defiance against Oda Nobunaga: the leading samurai commander in Japan at the time.

Stephen Turnbull

[1] Enya, Kikumi. 2021. *Ishiyama kassen wo yomi naosu*. Kyoto: Hōzōkan.

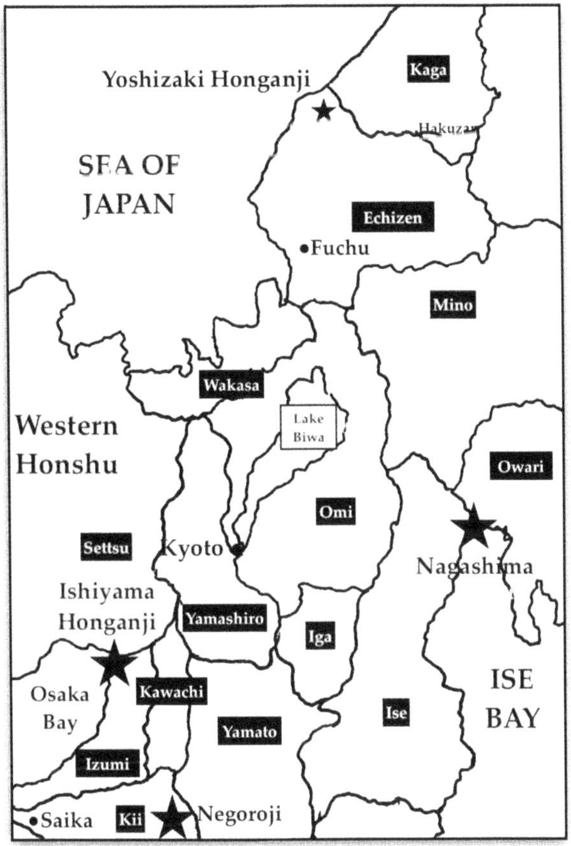

Map showing the provinces and other key places associated with the Ikko-ikki

The Ikkō-ikki
Art of War
as illustrated in
the military chronicles

1

The heroes of the Ishiyama Honganji

This picture introduces two key individuals whose very different influences helped to mould the Ikkō-ikki's Art of War Kennyo Kōsa (1543-92) (on the right) was the spiritual leader of the Honganji whose numerous calls to arms would be answered enthusiastically by the *monto*. Suzuki Shigehide (1546-86?) from the Saika-ikki in Kii Province, who placed his grasp of firearms technology at the service of Kennyo, is celebrated as the great layman samurai hero of the campaign. We see him here in 1582 as he dances, *naginata* in hand, in celebration of the news of the death of their deadliest enemy: Oda Nobunaga (EIKG 1,1).

2

Oda Nobunaga: enemy of the Ishiyama Honganji

Oda Nobunaga (1534-82), was always the greatest enemy of the Ikkō-ikki. A ruthless military genius who carried out the first stage of the reunification of Japan, Nobunaga would be responsible for several victories over the *monto* and their daimyo allies while perpetrating a number of severe massacres that would blacken his reputation forever. The Ikkō-ikki provided a serious military challenge to Nobunaga for ten years, helped by their religious commitment and the large scale deployment of firearms (EIKG 1,3).

3

The attack on the Ōtani Honganji by the sōhei of Enryakuji in 1465

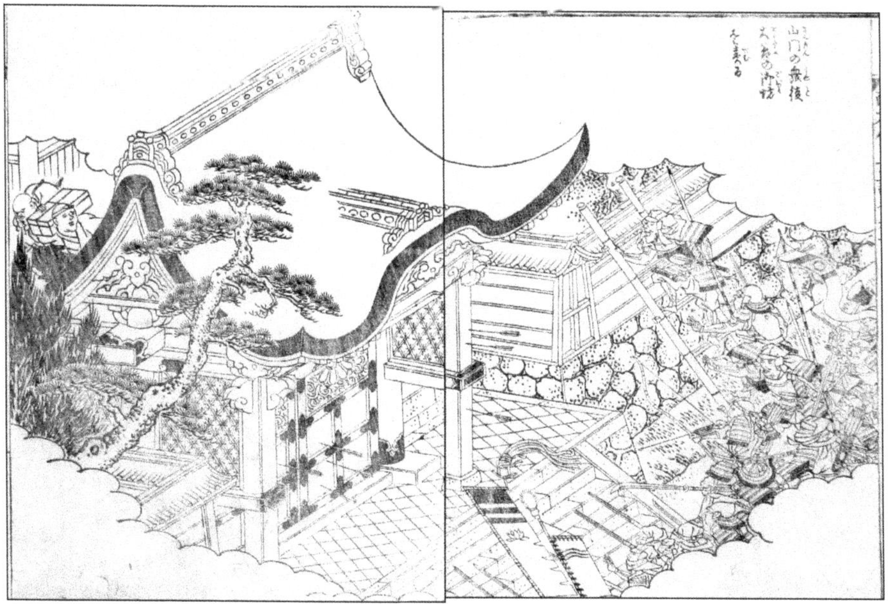

First we must go back in time to set the scene, because one hundred years before Nobunaga was born the Honganji branch of Jōdo-Shinshū was already experiencing violence from rival Buddhist sects. In 1465 Ōtani Honganji, their headquarters, was attacked and burned by *sōhei* from Enryakuji on Mount Hiei, who were enraged by the spread of Shinshū influence in Kyoto. As the classic example of genuine warrior monks, the aggressive *sōhei* are shown wearing their characteristic head cowls over their suits of armour. Their weapons are bows and *naginata* (ESSK 1,1).

4

Rennyo flees to Echizen

So great was the pressure from the Tendai sect of Mount Hiei and other sectarian opponents that in 1471 Rennyo, the current leader and great revivalist of Jōdo-Shinshū, was driven out of his first refuge in Wakasa Province and fled to Echizen, where he established a new Honganji headquarters called Yoshizaki Gobō. In this picture he is being welcomed to Echizen by local *monto*. An armed escort carrying a sheathed *naginata* guides them on to the path (EIKG 1,1).

5

The Ikkō-ikki of Kaga Province

Rennyo's establishment of a new Honganji in Echizen led to the expansion of its influence there and in the neighbouring province of Kaga, where the reputation for militancy of the Ikkō-ikki led to them being courted by the local daimyo Togashi Masachika. The *monto* eventually went to war on his behalf, but in 1488 they ousted Togashi and took over Kaga for themselves, ruling it independently for the next hundred years. In this picture the Kaga Ikkō-ikki have gathered noisily ready for war complete with a temple bell , conch trumpets and a huge drum. Their flags bear the invocation "Namu Amida Butsu":"Hail Amida Buddha" (ESSK 1,1).

6

The Kaga Ikkō-ikki in action (left hand panel)

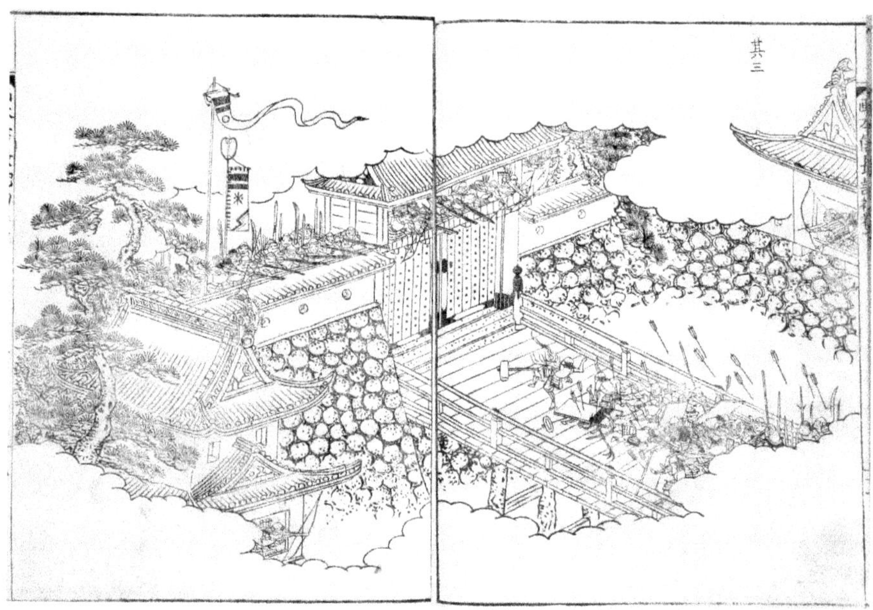

These two pictures are designed to be viewed as a continuous spread. They illustrate the Kaga Ikkō-ikki in action against an enemy castle at some unspecified date many years later, as shown by the inclusion of firearms. In the left hand panel the *monto* attack across the bridge against a hail of arrows and bullets, while the right hand panel displays the effects of cannon fire. (ESSK 1,1).

7

The Kaga Ikkō-ikki in action (right and panel)

The pictures are obviously meant to show the Ikkō-ikki as heroic lower class warriors armed with makeshift weapons and taking on a well-equipped samurai army. That would become the enduring image of the Ikkō-ikki's Art of War as it is depicted in the illustrated war chronicles. The leading *monto* who is crossing the bridge holding a mallet is hit by a bullet, while another man takes refuge from the gunfire under an upturned wooden rice tub (ESSK 1,1).

8

The destruction of the Yamashina Honganji in 1532

Rennyo returned to Kyoto in 1478 and founded the Yamashina Honganji to the east of the city as his new headquarters. From there the increasingly militant Ikkō-ikki carried out aggressive raids on sectarian rivals under the direction of their new leader Shōnyo (1516-64). Retaliation came in 1532 when the Yamashina Honganji was attacked and burned by supporters of the Nichiren sect along with sympathetic samurai allies from the Hosokawa and Rokkaku families (EIKG 1,2).

9

A conference of the monto is held inside the Ishiyama Honganji

Yearning for solitude, the ageing Rennyo had built a simple hermitage on the "long slope" that provided the name "Osaka", but by the time of his death in 1499 the devotion of his followers had ensured that there was to be little tranquility in that once remote location. Instead the new foundation called Ishiyama Honganji had grown into a large community. When Yamashina Honganji fell Rennyo's successor Shōnyo fled to this highly defensible strongpoint. It proved its worth by withstanding an attack in 1533, and remained the sect's headquarters from that time onwards (EIKG 1,5).

10

The Ikkō-ikki in action

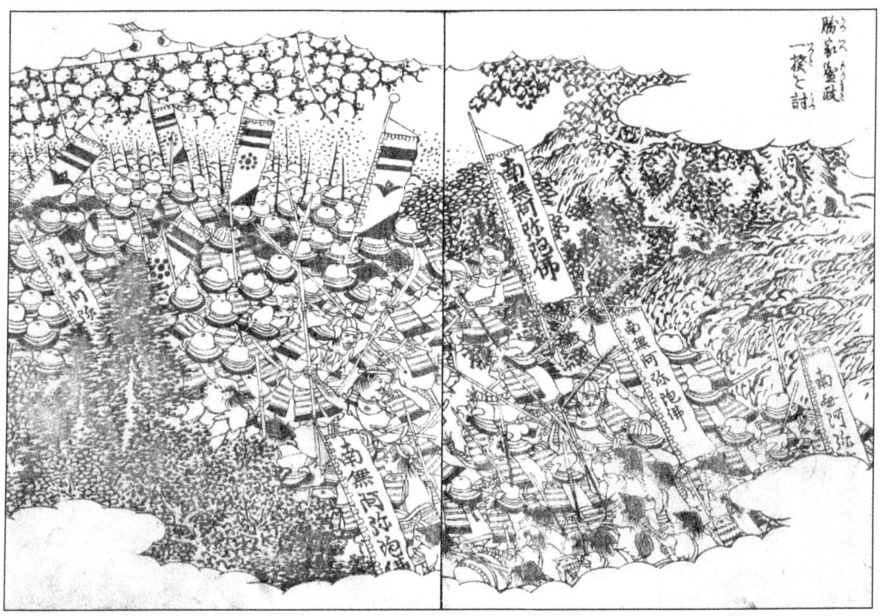

This picture from later on in the Ishiyama War presents a useful cameo of the Ikkō-ikki in action. They are attacking the rear ranks of Nobunaga's generals Sakuma Morimasa (1554-83; star motif) and Shibata Katsuie (1522-83; bird motif) . The ikki flags bear the six character *nenbutsu* "Namu Amida Butsu". They have spears, swords and *naginata* (ESSK 2,2).

11

The Saika-ikki go to war

Saika was an area of Kii province in what is now Wakayama City. During the Sengoku Period the majority of its inhabitants were adherents of the Ikkō sect, but they maintained a certain independence from the Honganji by organising themselves militarily as the Saika-ikki and operating largely as mercenaries, fighting for whom they wished. They were early users of firearms, but here we see them deploying a much more primitive missile weapon in the form of dropped stones (ESSK 2,2).

12

Oda Nobunaga's forces attack the Seiryūji

Oda Nobunaga's rise to power from comparative obscurity as the daimyo of Owari province to widespread recognition dates from his unexpected victory over Imagawa Yoshimoto at the battle of Okehazama in 1560. By 1568 he was able to march on Kyoto and install his own nominee Ashikaga Yoshiaki as the fifteenth (and last) Ashikaga shogun. Nobunaga's opponents were wide-ranging and included the Ikkō-ikki among other sectarian organisations. Here Nobunaga's army attack an obscure fortified position called the Seiryūji (ESSK 1,3).

13

Suzuki Shigehide fights Nobunaga at Hirano

In 1568 Nobunaga's crackdown on the Honganji began when he ordered its supporters not to supply rice to the headquarters. This attack on the inhabitants of Hirano in Ōmi province provides an instance of retaliation should a community not comply. Accompanying Nobunaga is Maeda Toshiie (1538-99) and Mori Yoshinari (1523-70). The Hirano force is noted as being led by Suzuki Magoichi Shigehide, the man who was to become a legendary hero of the Honganji army. His life and career have become much embellished by legend (EIKG 2,1).

14

Nobunaga attacks Tezutsuyama Castle

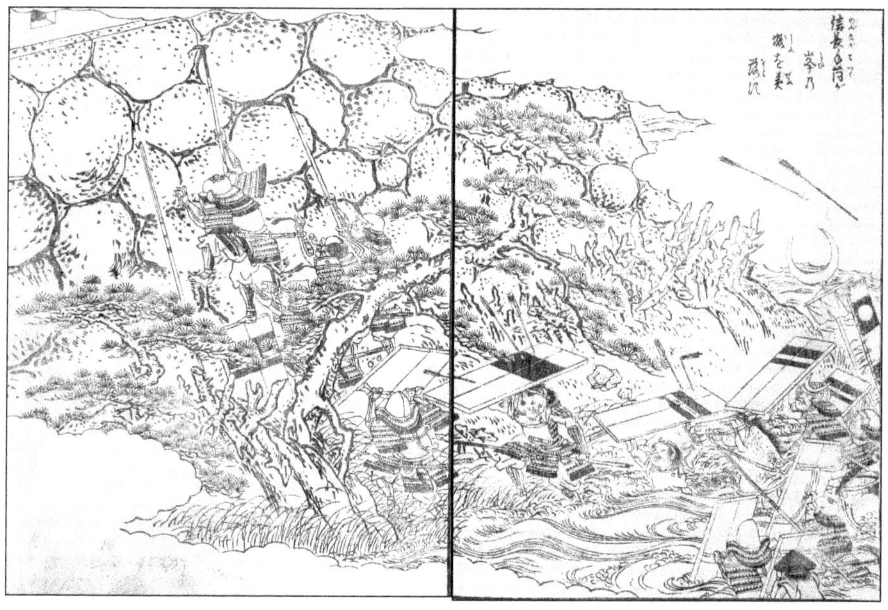

Foremost among Nobunaga's secular opponents was Asakura Yoshikage (1533-73) of Echizen province, for whom Tezutsuyama and Kanegasaki castle formed a single fortification system. Nobunaga captured the complex on 29 May 1570 and took 1,370 heads. The heartlands of Echizen province now lay open to him, but at that point Nobunaga's brother-in-law Azai Nagamasa (1545-73) of Ōmi turned against him and joined the Asakura. With his rear threatened, Nobunaga began a rapid retreat to Kyoto (ESSK 1,4).

15

A warrior monk makes an assassination attempt on Nobunaga

When Nobunaga was retreating through hostile Ōmi province on 22 June 1570 a monk called Sugitani Zenjubō attempted an assassination, but the shots merely grazed his victim. The account states that his gun fired a “double load”: a term commonly use in hunting, so Zenjubō is likely to have been a skilled and experienced marksman from the Saika-ikki, hired for the deed as a mercenary by the local daimyo Rokkaku Jōtei (EIKG 1,9).

16

Shibata Katsuie fights the Kaga Ikkō-ikki

Nobunaga's long campaigns against the Asakura and the Azai became thoroughly mixed up with various interventions against local Ikkō-ikki forces who joined the latter in an anti-Nobunaga coalition. Indeed, the Ikkō-ikki of Echizen and Kaga would provide opposition to Nobunaga throughout the time of the Ishiyama War and beyond. Here Nobunaga's general Shibata Katsuie goes into action against them during one of the earlier operations. In the foreground is his golden *gohei* standard copied from a Shinto priest's ritual prayer baton (EIKG 1, 8).

17

Kusunoki Masatomo joins the Ishiyama Honganji

The Ikkō-ikki attracted a wide range of supporters to their banner, and who better to swell the ranks of the army than a descendant of the famous samurai Kusunoki Masashige? When Oda Nobunaga invaded Ise province in 1567 Kusunoki Masatomo (1526-76) of Yuda castle helped in the resistance. The local daimyo Kitabatake Tomonori (1528-76) was defeated and was forced to adopt Nobunaga's son as his heir. Masatomo would not accept him as the heir, and went to Ishiyama Honganji along with his wife and children to offer his services to Kennyo (EIKG,1 7).

18

The fortifications of Noda and Fukushima

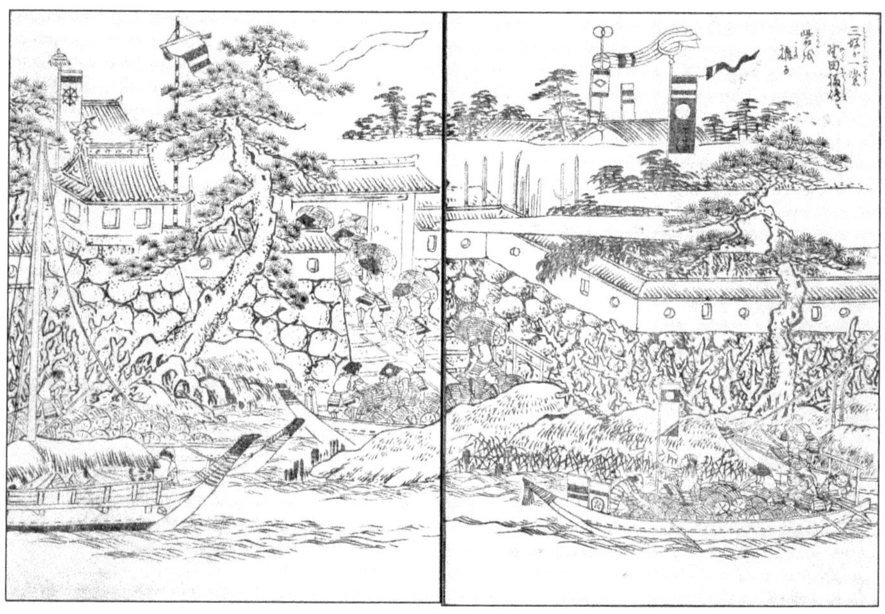

Among the key members of the first anti-Nobunaga coalition were three individuals of the Miyoshi clan known collectively as the Miyoshi Sanninshū (the Miyoshi "Triumvirs"). They fortified Noda and Fukushima, two castles in Settsu province located just to the north of the Ishiyama Honganji. The Miyoshi were well versed in the use of guns, having used them in their surprise night attack against the shogun's palace in 1565 when they killed Ashikaga Yoshiteru, and deployed them on a large scale in defence. Note now the forts are supplied from the river (ESSK 1,4).

19

Nobunaga sets out to fight the Miyoshi

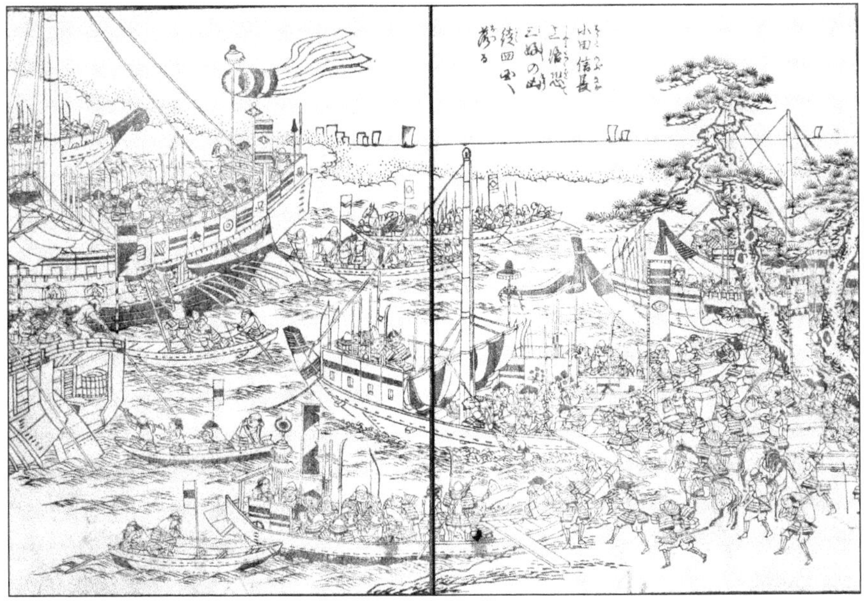

Bolstered by his victory over the Asakura and Azai at the battle of Anegawa in 1570 Nobunaga decided to take the fight directly to the Miyoshi Triumvirs. This picture shows Nobunaga's fleet loading up with troops and supplies. In reality his army moved overland, but the image illustrates how all the strong points of the Osaka Bay delta were dependent on rivers and seas for their defences and supplies. Armour chests are carried on board together with bales of rice (ESSK 1,2).

20

The Miyoshi Triumvirs awaits Nobunaga's attack at Noda and Fukushima

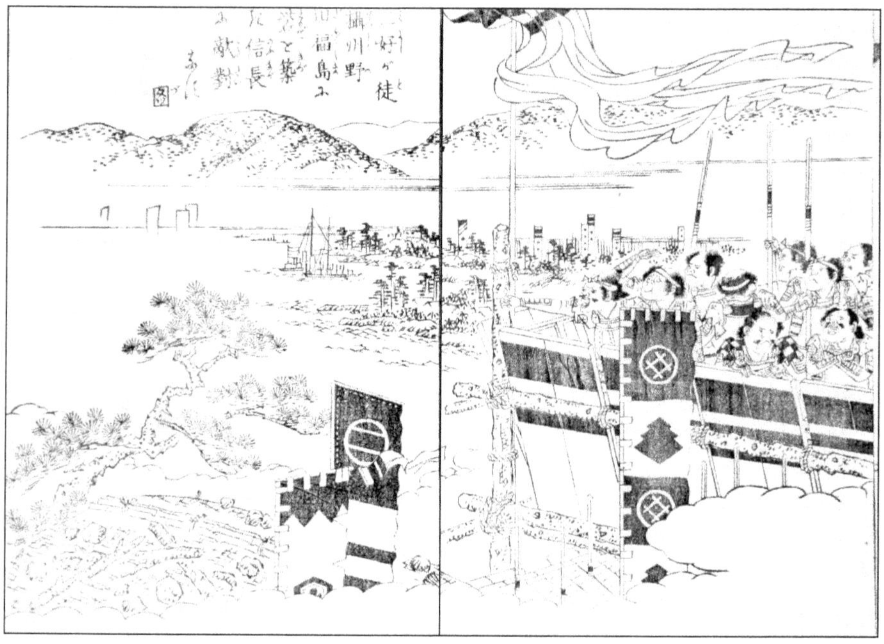

On 25 September 1570 Nobunaga began his attack on the forts of Noda and Fukushima. He was helped by friendly warrior monk mercenaries from Saika and the temple of Negoroji in Kii Province, who are supposed to have supplied 3,000 harquebuses. The thunder of friendly and of enemy guns "made heaven and earth shake night and day" said a chronicler about the fierce exchange of gunfire. Here the Miyoshi samurai in a crude lookout tower await anxiously the arrival of Nobunaga's fleet (EIKG 2,1).

21

The monto gather at Ishiyama Honganji

Nobunaga realised that if Noda and Fukushima fell then the Ishiyama Honganji would be very vulnerable. Accordingly he refused any negotiated settlement with the Miyoshi. Much alarmed by the battle taking place on his own doorstep Kennyo urged all sympathetic *monto* to join him in the Osaka Honganji and oppose Nobunaga. Here his supporters are doing just that (ESSK 1,4).

22

The monto assemble inside Ishiyama Honganji

As the fighting against Noda and Fukushima continued the Ikkō-ikki arrived at Ishiyama Honganji in large numbers. Here we see them being registered and relaxing with food and tobacco before the expected battle with Nobunaga. On the right is a banner bearing the nine character *nenbutsu*: "I take refuge in the Buddha of Inconceivable Light" (ESSK 1,4).

23

Envoys from the Asakura/Azai alliance meet Kennyo

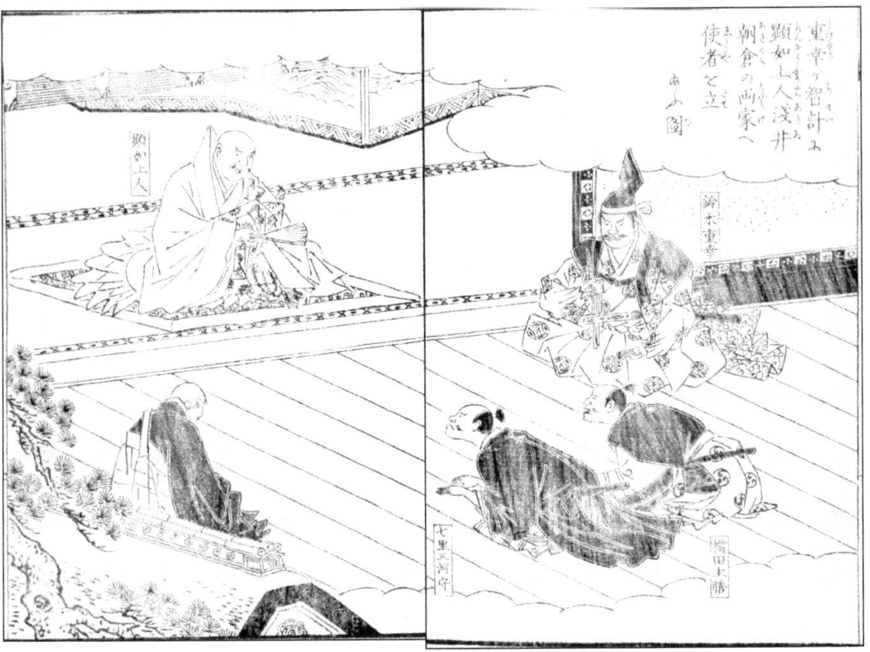

Reacting to rumours that Nobunaga was about to attack Ishiyama Honganji, Kennyo stepped up his ongoing negotiations with the Asakura and Azai early in October 1570. Here we see envoys from the alliance visiting Kennyo at Ishiyama Honganji while Suzuki Shigehide looks on. Within days Kennyo would order his followers to attack Nobunaga's positions around Osaka.(EIKG 2,2).

24

Harvesting the rice crop for the Honganji under the protection of gunfire

On 8 October 1570 Nobunaga moved his headquarters to Tenmagamori, from where he could threaten the Ishiyama Honganji just across the river. Here the Ikkō-ikki rush to gather in their precious ripened rice crop from the fields owned by Ishiyama Honganji's general Shimotsuma Rairyū (1552-1609) under the cover of harquebus fire (EIKG 2,2).

25

Oda Nobunaga lays in supplies

In preparation for his attack against Ishiyama Honganji Nobunaga's position receives supplies. Farmers bring in bales of rice and large individual fish in baskets. Nobunaga's *mon* (badge) appears on the *maku* (field curtains). Note the simple sharpened bamboo defences above the crude gate (ESSK 1, 4).

26

The Ishiyama War is launched when the Ikkō-ikki make a night attack on Nobunaga's camp

The Ishiyama War began in earnest in the middle of the night of 13 October 1570 when the Honganji commenced hostilities against Nobunaga by firing guns at his outlying positions. Nobunaga was taken completely by surprise. Here we see harquebuses blasting their shots into the night sky, their targets identified only by the light from the camp fires of Shibata Katsuie's troops. Disciplined gunfire like this would become a characteristic feature of the Ishiyama War (ESSK,1,4).

27

Suzuki Shigehide builds a dyke

The following pictures illustrate a clever stratagem credited to Suzuki Shigehide. It is probably complete fiction, but the story draws on similar authentic operations conducted elsewhere; Hideyoshi became famous for the tactic. Under Shigehide's direction the Ikkō-ikki are building a dyke that will be used to flood Nobunaga's camp (ESSK 1,4).

28

The monto flood Nobunaga's camp

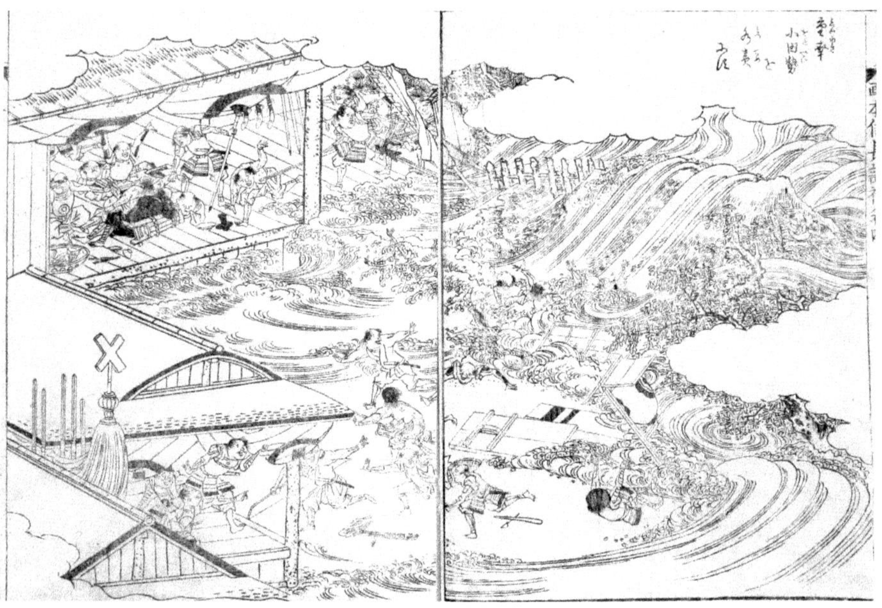

At the given moment the dyke is cut and flood waters rush into Nobunaga's position. Certain historical sources claim that a similar tactic was used against Nobunaga at Nagashima in 1571, where the Ikkō-ikki broke the dyke that had long protected the land where Nobunaga's army was encamped (ESSK 1,4).

29

The flood 1

The Ikkō-ikki take to boats to harass Nobunaga's troops still further. Two soldiers reload their harquebuses. Others spear their victims who have fallen into the water (ESSK 1,4).

30

The flood 2

This pair of pictures are designed to be viewed a continuous whole. The survivors of the flood cling to dry land as the waters wash even horses away (ESSK 1,4).

31

The flood 3

Supported by Ikkō-ikki marksmen on land, the boatmen in their straw raincoats kill more of Nobunaga's troops. Nobunaga's *mon* appears on a floating shield. (ESSK 1,4).

32

An attack on the Ishiyama Honganji

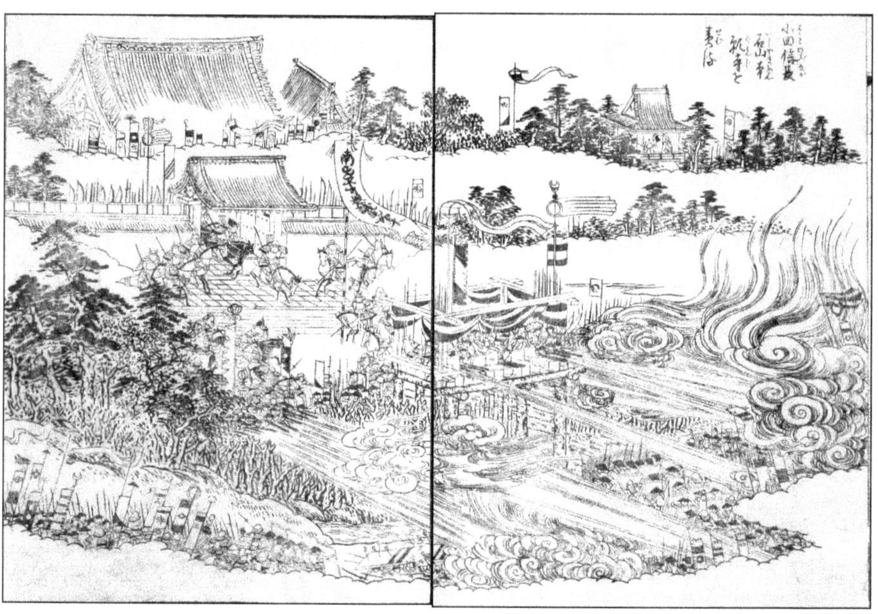

This picture provides a far more likely scenario for Nobunaga's assault on Ishiyama Honganji. The specifically religious buildings of the fortified temple are seen to the rear. Guns blaze out from both sides as Nobunaga attacks the main gate across one of the water courses. Note the crude "barbican" extension to the gateway built hurriedly from undressed timber (ESSK 1,5).

33

Suzuki Magoichi Shigehide counter-attacks

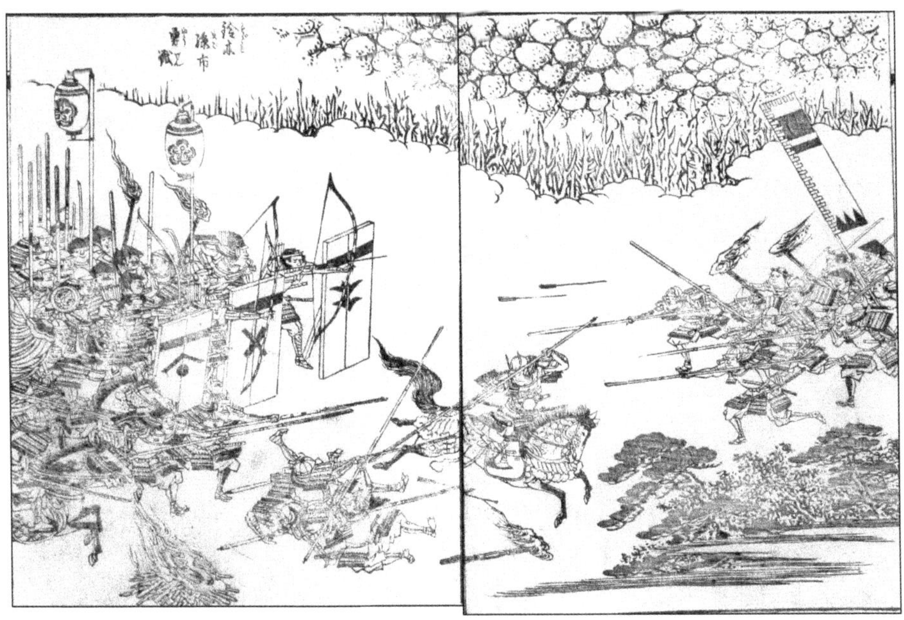

With flaming pine torches providing light, Suzuki Shigehide leads the Ikkō-ikki in a counter-attack against Nobunaga under the cover of darkness. The Oda lines are illuminated by a bonfire and by paper lanterns bearing Nobunaga's *mon.* Spear fighting predominates in this particular encounter (ESSK 1,5).

34

Nobunaga's army flee

Driven back from the gates of Ishiyama Honganji, Nobunaga's armies withdraw. The artist has conveyed the panic very well. A senior samurai wearing a face mask and holding a pine torch guides his men to safety. One bears a heavy harquebus across his shoulder. From this time on Nobunaga would concentrate on the numerous outlying positions of the Ikkō-ikki and those of their allies rather than attempting another costly major assault on the inner citadel (ESSK 1,5).

35

Toyotomi Hideyoshi and Suzuki Shigehide

Nobunaga's most loyal and successful general was Toyotomi Hideyoshi (1537-98), who would one day succeed him as the second unifier of Japan. On 27 January 1571 Nobunaga ordered Hideyoshi to cut off all supply routes between Echizen and Osaka and thus break the physical link in the anti-Nobunaga alliance. Here Hideyoshi is juxtaposed with Suzuki Shigehide of the ikki forces. Hideyoshi's famous "thousand gourd standard" flies above him (EIKG 2,3).

36

The first action by the Nagashima Ikkō-ikki against Nobunaga leads to the death of his brother Oda Nobuoki at Kokie castle

The other main base of the Ikkō-ikki lay in the Nagashima Delta. Nobunaga's war against it took four years and cost the lives of four of his close relatives, of whom the first victim was his younger brother Nobuoki, who built a castle at Kokie. In their initial action against Nobunaga, the local ikki took advantage of the distraction provided by the Asakura/Azai campaign and attacked it. Nobuoki was forced to commit suicide on 18 December 1570. Here the astonished yet satisfied *monto* look across as his castle blazes. Two are shown as cowled warriors (ESSK 1,7).

37

The Nagashima Ikkō-ikki fire on Nobunaga's army at the Ōta-guchi

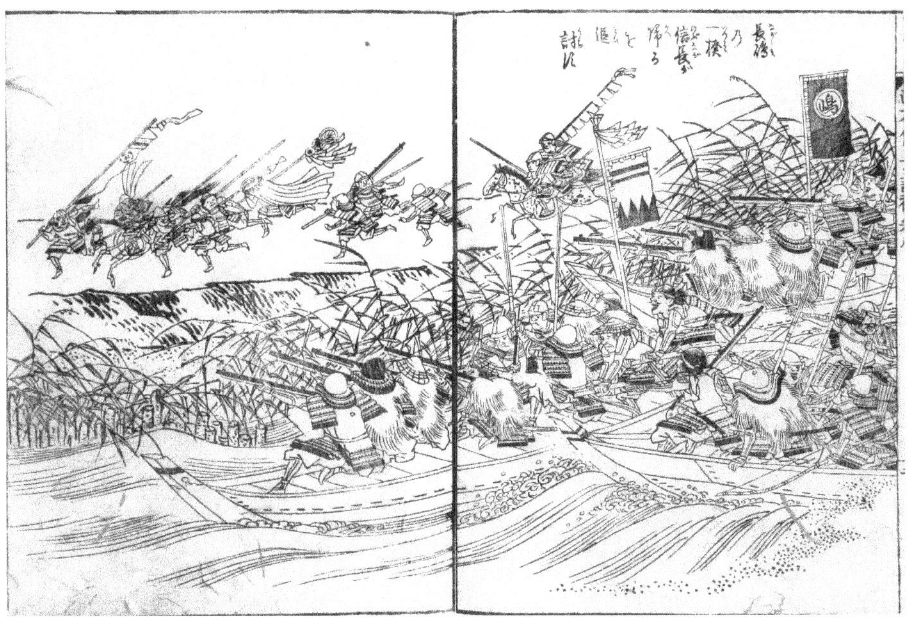

Nobunaga replied by launching his first campaign against the Nagashima Ikkō-ikki on 4 June 1571, but after setting fire to various places he prudently began to withdraw. The ikki then counter-attacked, exploiting the terrain of a number of low-lying islands where several rivers met, where the Ikkō-ikki settlements were built on *wajū:* flatlands protected from the waters by dykes or levees. The most serious damage was inflicted upon the unit of Nobunaga's army that withdrew via the Ōta-guchi (Ōta approach), where they were forced to move in single file (ESSK 1,8).

38

Ujiie Bokuzen Naomoto is killed at the Ōta-guchi

The Nagashima Ikkō-ikki's counterattack against Nobunaga began on 8 June 1571, by firing bows and harquebuses from within the numerous water courses within the reed plains as their enemies proceeded along the narrow dyke. Shibata Katsuie was slightly wounded and withdrew. In ta subsequent encounter the general Ujiie Bokuden Naomoto was killed. Here he is shown in action against the crudely armoured *monto* (ESSK 1,8).

39

Yuge Shurisuke fights to the last at Nagashima

Ujiie Naomoto suffered numerous casualties among his men, including his retainer Yuge Shurisuke who was forced to commit suicide at Ōta-guchi after fighting bravely against the *monto*. One of his opponents has dropped his war drum. Most are wearing straw raincoats against the downpour. With this action Nobunaga's first Nagashima campaign came to an ignominious end (ESSK 1,8).

40

A battle with the monto at Kamanoha castle

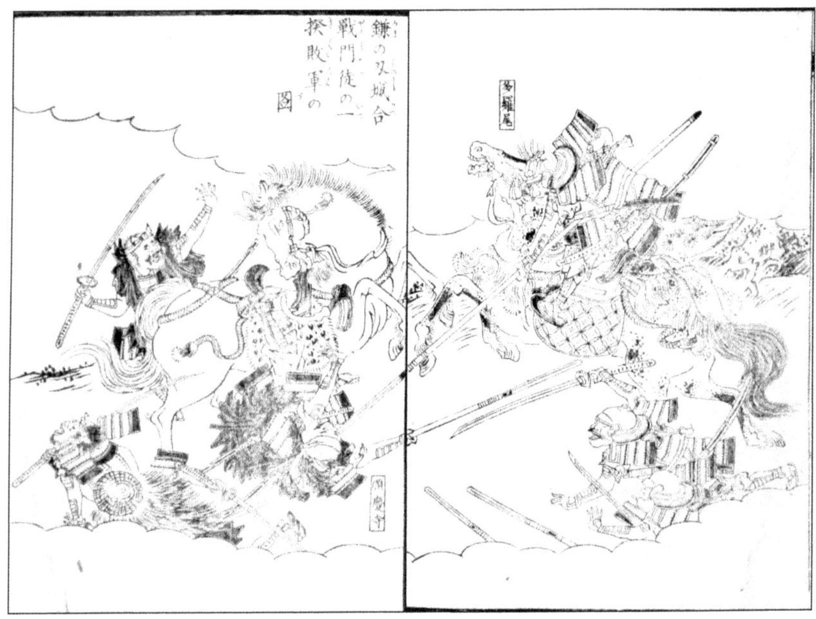

Kamanoha was a border castle established by the Azai whose keeper had defected to Nobunaga's side in 1570. In June 1571, at about the same time as the Nagashima operation, a striking force under Azai Shichirō assaulted it. Here one of Nobunaga's samurai identified only as Tarao fights Azai's Ikkō-ikki allies at Kamanoha. Two of them are depicted as shaven-headed Buddhist priests from the Junkeiji temple (EIKG 2,3).

41

The Asakura and Azai troops are succoured by the monks of Mount Hiei

A year earlier in October 1570, Nobunaga had defeated an Asakura/Azai army at Sakamoto in Ōmi province. The village lay at the foot of Mount Hiei, with whose inhabitants the troops of the Asakura and Azai then sought refuge, and the warrior monks of the Enryakuji welcomed them. It was a fateful mistake for their hosts to make, and in 1571 a terrible retribution came their way (ETKK, 4,1).

42

Oda Nobunaga attacks Mount Hiei

Seemingly surrounded by enemies in the anti-Nobunaga coalition, Oda Nobunaga decided to make a serious gesture as a warning to all by punishing the monks of Mount Hiei who had succoured his enemies, but the operation proved to be much more than a mere gesture. Instead Nobunaga attacked Mount Hiei and its numerous temples with ruthless overwhelming force. Marksmen with harquebuses scoured the area and shot down people indiscriminately. Here only the simplest of defences in the form of wooden shields protect the holy temple (ESSK 1,8)

43

Nobunaga's samurai kill the monks of the Enryakuji

This picture shows the fine details of the slaughter on Mount Hiei that would blacken Nobunaga's name forever. His men made their way up the forested mountain from several directions, slaughtering the inhabitants and burning buildings. Tens of thousand of people are believed to have been killed, and the famous warrior monks of Mount Hiei were no more (ETK 2,6).

Kennyo performs a Buddhist ritual for his followers

Throughout the time of the Ishiyama War Kennyo kept up his role as the spiritual leader of the Ikkō-ikki. For a religiously motivated army these gestures were every bit as important as gaining military victories. In this picture he is conducting a memorial service for the slain (ESSK 1,4).

45

Toyotomi Hideyoshi fights the Miyoshi clan

In this picture Toyotomi Hideyoshi uses concentrated harquebus fire against the troops of the Miyoshi clan as they cross a river. This action was part of Nobunaga's strategy of "divide and conquer" against the hostile alliance (ESSK 1,6).

46

An ambush takes place

In this picture an army is ambushed and defeated amid a hail of stones dropped from above. The caption is ambiguous, because the gourd standard would appear to suggest that Hideyoshi is the victim at the hands of the Ikkō-ikki, not the reverse (ESSK 1,6).

47

The warrior monks of Heisenji 1573

The Heisenji was a temple in Echizen province belonging to the Tendai sect of Mount Hiei. It was a centre for mountain worship and one of the places traditionally used to commence an ascent of the holy mountain of Hakuzan. Like their counterparts at the Enryakuji the Heisenji maintained a force of warrior monks, but when faced with Nobunaga in 1573 they soon abandoned their support for the Asakura and joined forces with him (ESSK 1,9).

48

Keya Shichirōza'emon holds the line as Nobunaga withdraws from Nagashima

Nobunaga's second Nagashima campaign in the autumn of 1573 was as much of a failure as the first, and his forces were harassed by the Nagashima Ikkō-ikki as they withdrew from northern Ise. The firearms of both sides were useless because of heavy rain, but local supporters of the Honganji from Iga and Kōka kept up a steady barrage of arrows. Keya Shichirōza'emon made repeated charges against the enemy to allow Nobunaga to regroup and eventually reach the safety of Ōgaki castle (ESSK 1,4).

Nobunaga visits Nara to collect a sample of rare incense wood

This remarkable incident has no direct connection with the Ishiyama War but demonstrates the hold that Nobunaga had over the imperial court and the religious establishment. A very rare block of fragrant incense wood had been kept in the imperial storehouse of the Shoso-In at Nara for over 800 years. Nobunaga haughtily demanded a piece, which was supplied among great ritual and pomp on 19 April 1574. Nobunaga thus became one of only three people in the whole of Japanese history who have shared the wood, thus proclaiming his assumed status as a man equivalent in rank to the shogun (EIKG 2,4).

50

Oda Nobunaga's final campaign against the Nagashima Ikkō-ikki

Nobunaga's final campaign against Nagashima Ikkō-ikki was launched on 30 June 1574. Various units of his large army made simultaneous attacks from different directions into the delta. Here we see the two armies standing off across the river between two *wajū*. The banner flying with Nobunaga's army is not the *nenbutsu* but that of the rival Nichiren Sect: "Hail to the Lotus of the Divine Law" (ESSK 1,9).

51

The battle of Nagashima, 1574

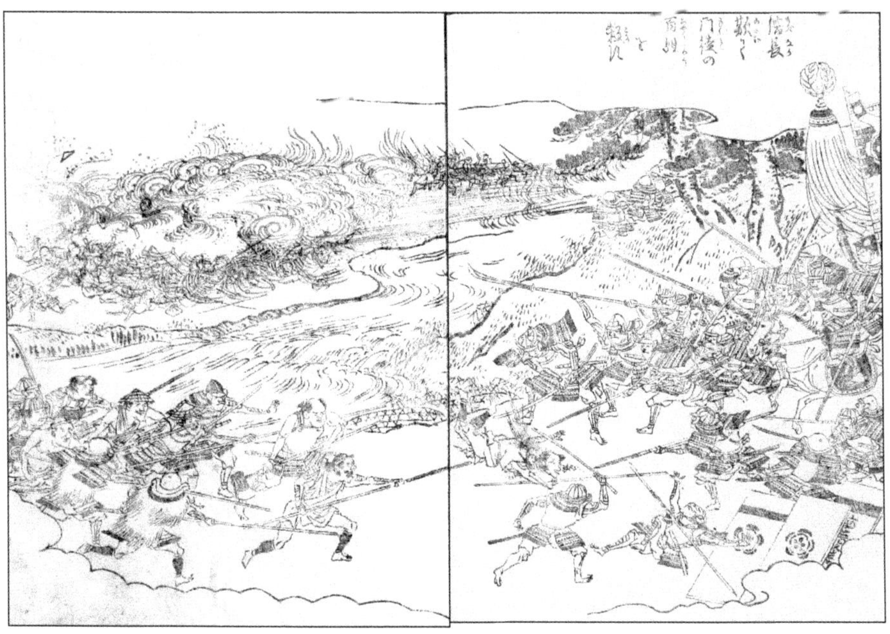

Nobunaga's army attacked deeply into the *wajū* , supported by ships out in the bay. Large-bored harquebuses were brought up and fired into the forts. Nobunaga initially refused quarter, although one or two of the ikki forts surrendered and their garrisons joined his army. Here the Ikkō-ikki make a brave assault (ESSK 1,9).

52

The massacre of the Nagashima Ikkō-ikki

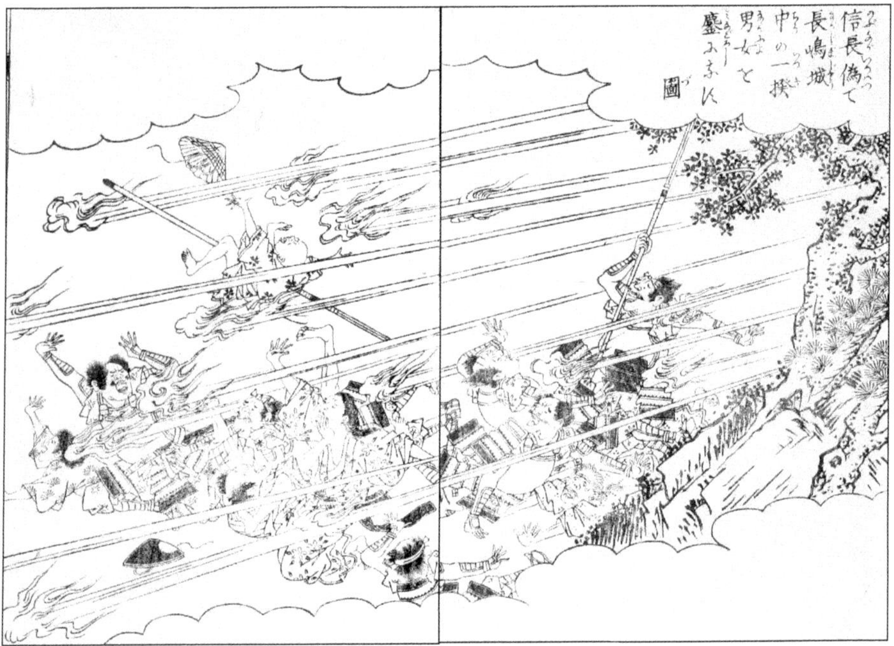

The capture of all the Ikko-ikki outposts on the mainland cut off Nagashima from help, and under sustained gunfire the remaining Ikkō-ikki crammed themselves into the two fortresses of Nakae and Yanagashima. Waiting until the weather was dry and a suitable wind was blowing, Nobunaga's men piled up brushwood against the outer buildings and set fire to the entire place, burning everyone to death. (EIKG 2,5).

53

Katsurada Nagatoshi (aka Maeba Yoshitsugu) is attacked by the Honganji ikki

When Nobunaga defeated the Asakura in 1573 he appointed Maeba Yoshitsugu as his governor of Echizen, but by 1574 Yoshitsugu's treatment of his peers was giving such concern that they revolted against him. This prompted the local Ikkō-ikki to join in, and with their help Nobunaga's forces were driven out of Echizen. Here we see the unfortunate Yoshitsugu being overcome by a group of *monto* in a very personal act of *gekokujō* ("the low overcome the high") (ESSK 1,8).

54

Nobunaga invades Echizen and Kaga province to destroy the Ikkō-ikki

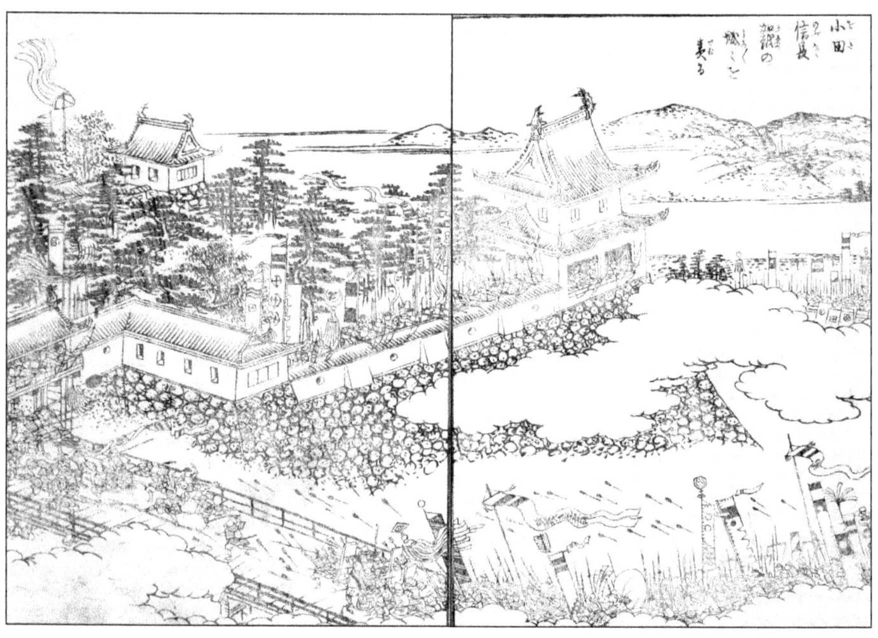

Oda Nobunaga had gained Echizen from the Asakura clan only to see it slip from his grasp again at the hands of the Ikkō-ikki. In 1575, with his confidence bolstered by having vanquished Nagashima, Nobunaga turned his attention once again to subjugating the Ikkō-ikki of Echizen and Kaga in a campaign that would exceed even Nagashima in its cruelty and ferocity (ESSK 1,10).

55

People flee to the mountains of Echizen as Nobunaga's armies approach

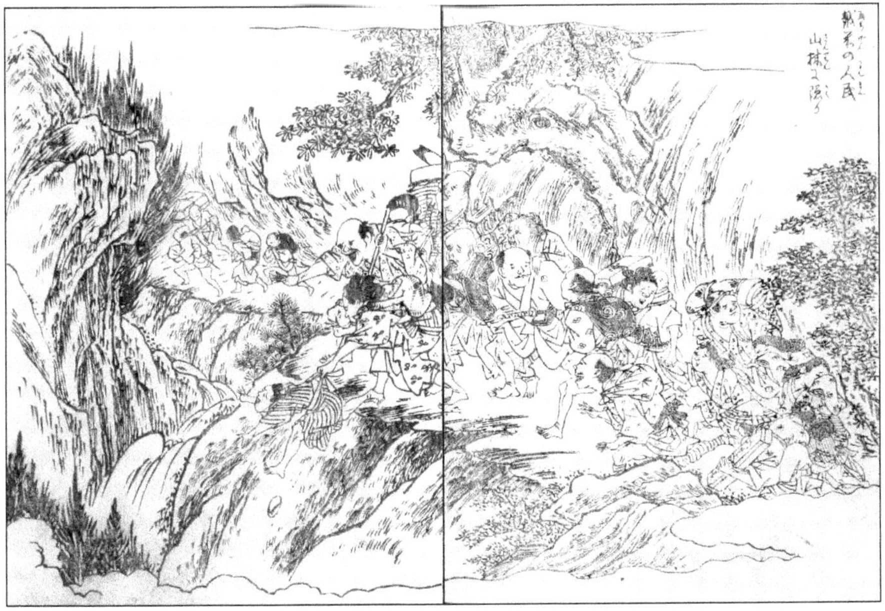

Fearful of experiencing the same fate as the civilians of Nagashima, the people of Echizen fled to the mountains. Nobunaga would later boast that he had slaughtered tens of thousands of these "vermin" at the town of Fuchū alone (ESSK 1,10).

56

Shibata Katsuie executes Ikkō-ikki prisoners in Echizen

The refugees' fears proved justified when Shibata Katsuie began executing prisoners by the score. Nevertheless, resistance continued in Echizen and Kaga for the entire time of the Ishiyama War and beyond until the year of Nobunaga's death. The fort of Torigoe, for example, had changed hands several times by 1582 (EIKG 2,2).

57

Shimotsuma Raishō is captured by the rival Takada-ikki

Nobunaga may have been ruthless, but he was also a skilful politician, and this picture illustrates how he was able to play off different factions within Jōdo-Shinshū against each other. One rival grouping were the Takada branch in Echizen, whose hostility to the dominant Honganji branch led them in 1575 to capture Shimotsuma Raishō (1516-75), the Honganji's governor of Echizen, on Nobunaga's behalf (ESSK 1,10).

58

Akechi Mitsuhide fights Suzuki Shigehide

With Echizen seemingly under control, Nobunaga commenced another siege of the Ishiyama Honganji in May 1575 when he sent 10,000 troops against the Osaka complex. They swept up the remnants of the Miyoshi and Asakura forces on the way. Here Suzuki Shigehide is juxtaposed with Akechi Mitsuhide (1528-82), who was one of Nobunaga's most reliable generals in the fight against the Honganji, but was also the man who would ultimately betray him (EIKG 2,2).

Harquebuses are fired from Ishiyama Honganji against the troops of Sakuma Morimasa

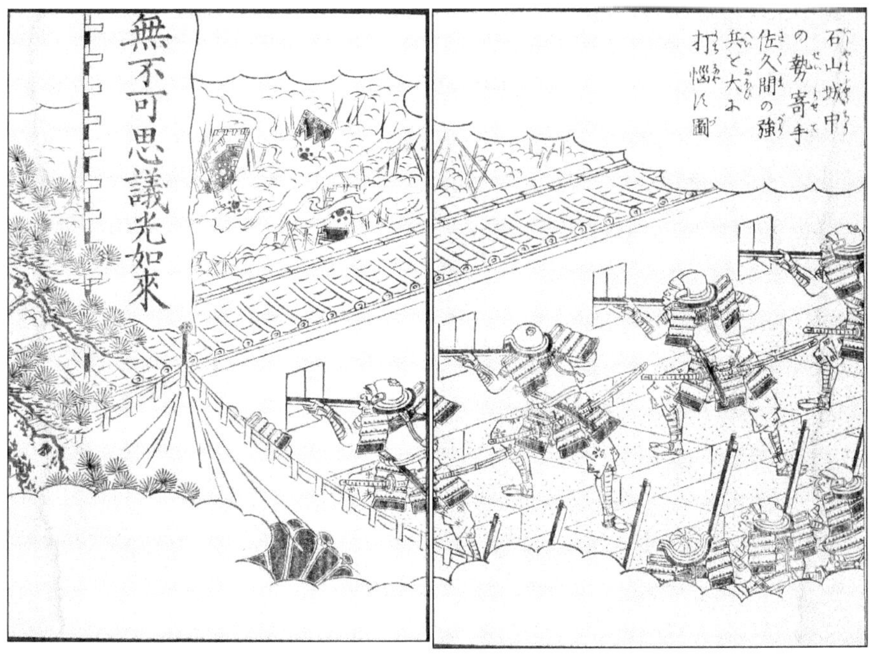

Here we see an excellent image of the defence of Ishiyama Honganji in 1575 using firearms. Neat ranks of harquebusiers wait to take the place of their comrades firing a volley through the loopholes. The first character on their flag is missing, but otherwise it shows us the clearest depiction yet of the nine character invocation: "I take refuge in the Buddha of Inconceivable Light" (EIKG 2,6).

60

Prayers are exchanged across the moat of Ishiyama Honganji

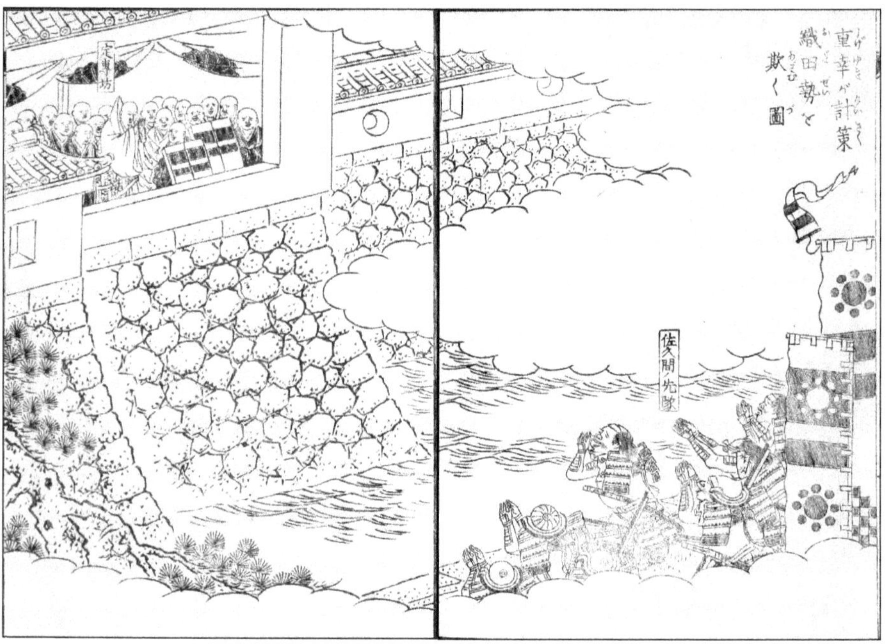

Belief in Amida Buddha and the power of the *nenbutsu* was not confined to members of the Ikkō-ikki faction, as this fascinating picture illustrates. The Osaka Honganji is under siege from the troops of Sakuma Morimasa, but a priest has persuaded the attacking vanguard, who are obviously also believers in the tenets of Jōdo-Shinshū, to join him in reciting the *nenbutsu*. Such incidents would give Nobunaga great concern for his soldiers' morale and primary allegiance (EIKG 2,6).

61

Suzuki Shigehide tries to assassinate Oda Nobunaga

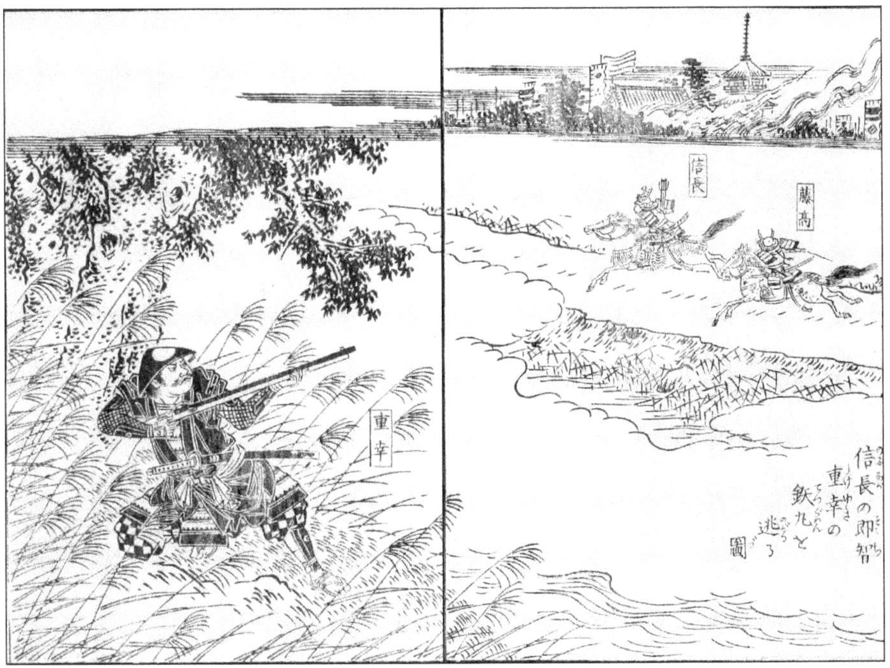

Among the accomplishments credited by legend to the hero Suzuki Shigehide was an attempt to shoot Nobunaga. He lay in wait as a sniper until Nobunaga came riding past. Once again, Nobunaga survived (EIKG 2,6)

62

Suzuki Shigehide inspires his son Suzuki Toyondo

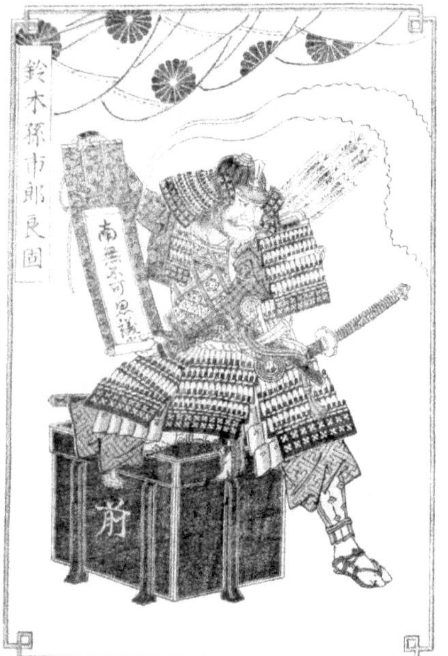

This pair of portraits introduce us to Suzuki Shigehide's legendary and heroic son Suzuki Toyondo. Here Shigehide shows him how the words of the *nenbutsu* can ensure his triumph over his enemies. The invocation of Amida is accompanied by a vision of Shinran (EIKG 2,1).

63

Suzuki Toyondo uses the power of Amida's name to defeat Kobayashi Danzō

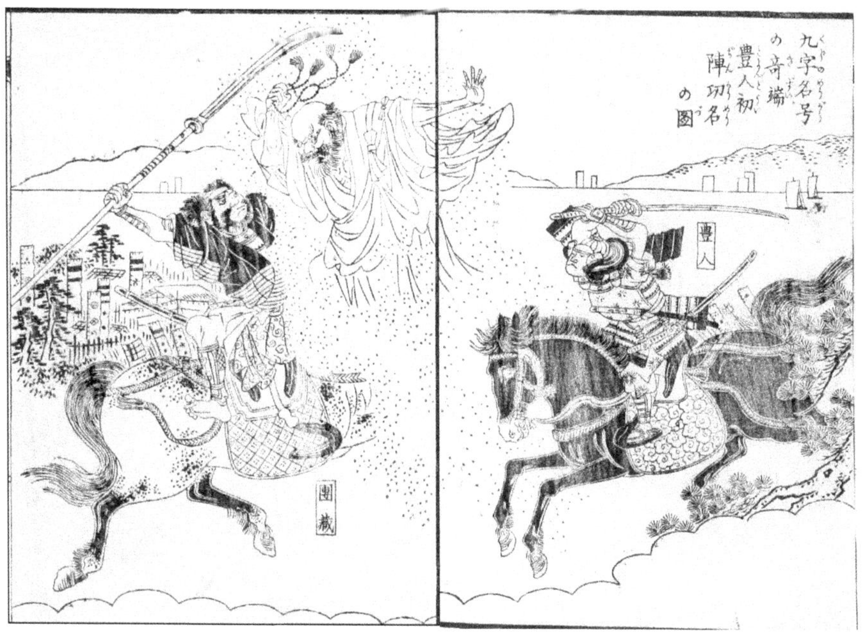

This remarkable picture anthropomorphises the *nenbutsu*. Fighting in his first battle, Suzuki Toyondo is challenged by a samurai called Kobayashi Danzō. Toyondo utters the nine character *nenbutsu* and it takes the shape of a terrifying holy man. Danzō falls back in defeat, with his useless *naginata* clutched in his hand (EIKG 2,7)

64

The battle at Fort Kizu in 1576

In 1576 Nobunaga ordered a further operation against Ishiyama Honganji and its outlying forts. On 30 May his army attacked Fort Kizu, but about 10,000 *monto* advanced from Osaka and Rōnokishi in support of their comrades and blasted the attackers with heavy gunfire from supposedly thousands of harquebuses, leaving several senior commanders dead including Ban Naomasa, who was killed outside Fort Mitsudera (ESSK 1,12).

65

Suzuki Shigehide attacks Fort Tennōji

The *monto* under Shigehide then assaulted Nobunaga's own base at Tennōji. On 1 June Nobunaga set off to relieve Tennoji and attacked from the direction of Sumiyoshi. To encourage his men he made himself very conspicuous, riding up and down and giving orders, when a harquebus bullet hit him in the leg. Nothing daunted, Nobunaga advanced again under heavy gunfire and relieved Tennōji, after which he led a pursuit as far as the gates of Ishiyama Honganji itself (ESSK 1,9)

66

Nobunaga's guard ships ride at anchor in Osaka Bay

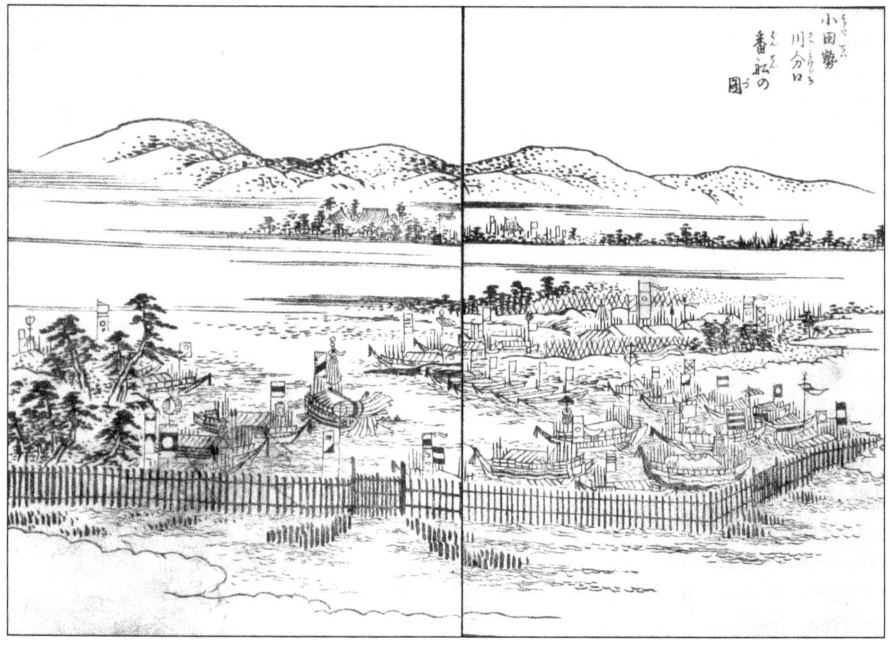

Ishiyama Honganji was supplied from the sea by the Mōri clan of the Inland Sea area where they ruled supreme. Hoping to cut off the supply line, Nobunaga placed guard ships in Osaka Bay, protected by a fence linking the islands (EIKG 2,8).

67

The First Battle of Kizugawaguchi, 1576

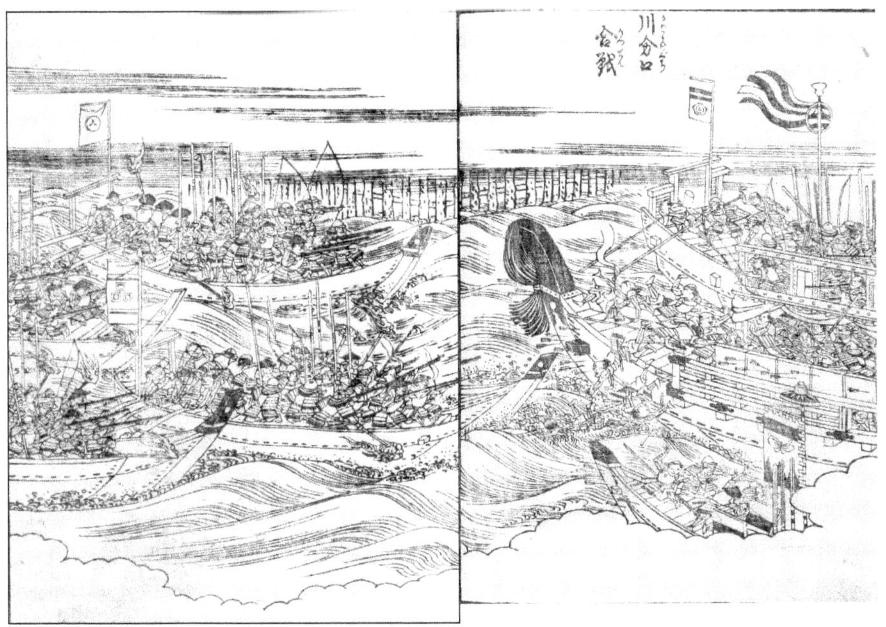

Challenging Nobunaga's attempted blockade, the Mōri brought up warships to fight Nobunaga in 1576 at the mouth of the Kizu River in what became known as the first battle of Kizugawaguchi (ESSK 1,13).

68

The name of Amida Buddha calms the tempestuous waves

In this symbolic picture of sea fighting the *nenbutsu* calms even the tempestuous waves. Note the *mon* (badge) of the sympathetic Mōri clan on the bows of the ship(EIKG 2,8).

69

Hand to hand fighting takes place at the first Battle of Kizugawaguchi

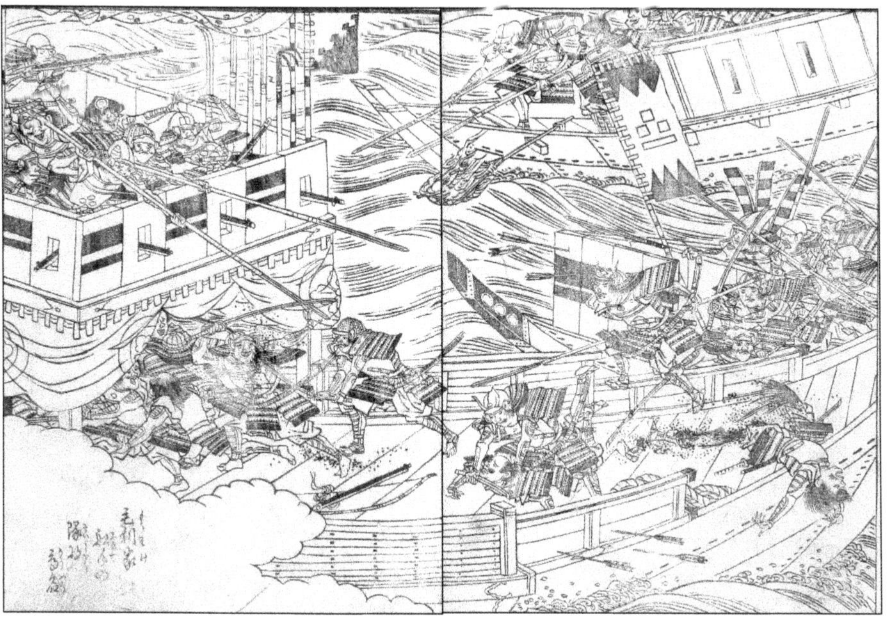

Here the battle of Kizugawaguchi is at its height as Mōri's superior craft collide with Nobunaga's ships. Arrows, bullets (and bombs, which are not shown here) rain down on the decks and break Nobunaga's blockade. Hand to hand fighting is however still the key to victory. One man has his legs cut off while another loses his head as a trophy. Note the basket of fire on a pole (ESSK 2,1).

70

Nobunaga's army is attacked on land at the same time as the battle of Kizugawaguchi

Fighting also took place on land while the Kizugawaguchi battle raged at sea. Encouraged by what was going on out on the waves, the Ikkō-ikki garrisons in the outlying forts of Osaka sallied out and attacked Nobunaga's besieging armies (EIKG 1,11).

71

Soldiers disguised as Honganji warriors sneak into the rear of Shigisan castle

Oda Nobunaga's campaigns against the hostile alliance were not helped by a number of defections among certain of his senior officers. Matsunaga Hisahide (1508-77) was one such traitor. He abandoned Nobunaga and shut himself up in Shigisan castle. Fierce retribution followed and Hisahide was killed. Here Nobunaga's forces are entering the castle in secret disguised as Honganji supporters. (EIKG 2,10).

72

Nobunaga's envoys engage in peace talks with Kennyo at Ishiyama Honganji

The war against the Ishiyama Honganji was interrupted by several periods of truce. Here is one instance where peace talks between Kennyo and Nobunaga's representative led to another temporary cessation of hostilities (EIKG 3,1).

Suzuki Shigehide experiences a divine revelation

This is another religiously-themed picture that shows the devotion to Jōdo-Shinshū that was at the heart of Suzuki Shigehide's commitment to the Honganji cause. Watched by his comrade Shimotsuma Nakataka (1551-1616; the son of Shimotsuma Raishō), Shigehide experiences a divine revelation (EIKG 3,1).

74

Suzuki Shigehide composes a farewell poem en route to the battlefield

Suzuki Shigehide was a true samurai as well as a *monto*. Thinking that his next encounter would be his last battle because of the divine revelation he had just received, Shigehide composed a farewell poem in the manner of the warriors of old on his way to the battlefield (EIKG 3,1).

75

Hideyoshi fights Suzuki at Onohara

Here Toyotomi Hideyoshi meets Suzuki Shigehide in battle once again outside the fort of Onohara in the Osaka area (EIKG 3,2).

76

An attack on the Ishiyama Honganji - 1

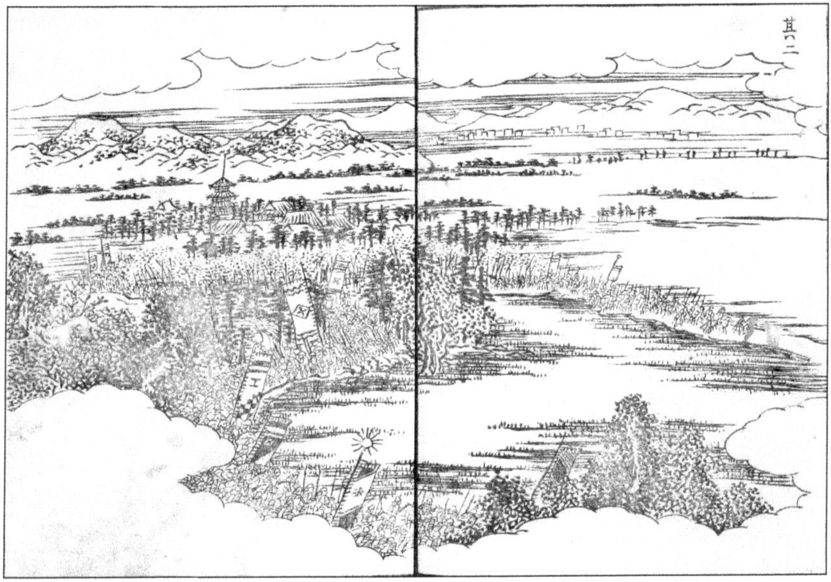

This dramatic pair of pictures shows a panoramic view of one of Nobunaga's later attacks on the Ishiyama Honganji. Here his vast army makes its way between the rivers and islands (ESSK 2,2).

77

An attack on the Ishiyama Honganji - 2

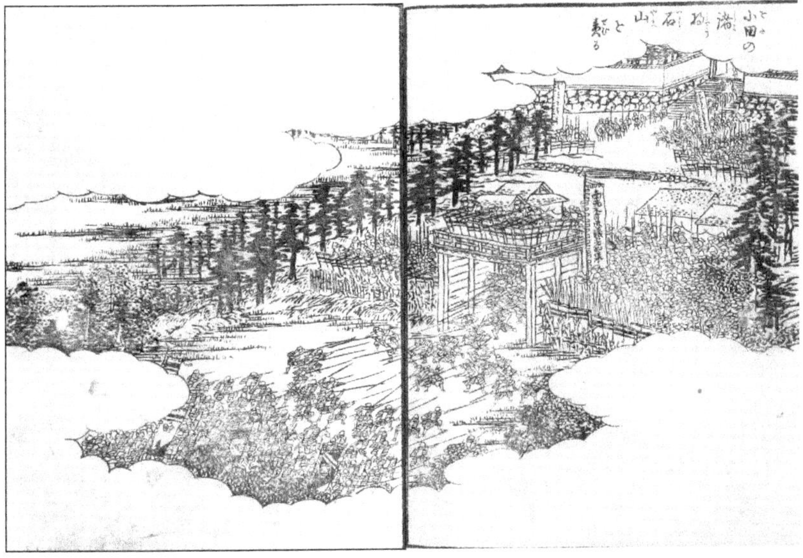

The right hand panel shows the main gate under attack. The outer gateway is reinforced using densely packed wooden shields. Nobunaga's samurai attack with lowered spears (ESSK 2,2).

78

The army of the Ishiyama Honganji counter attack Nobunaga

In this picture the Ikkō-ikki army rally and take the attack back to Nobunaga. Once more firearms are heavily involved (ESSK 2,2).

79

The Ikkō-ikki evacuate Fort Kaizuka in Izumi province

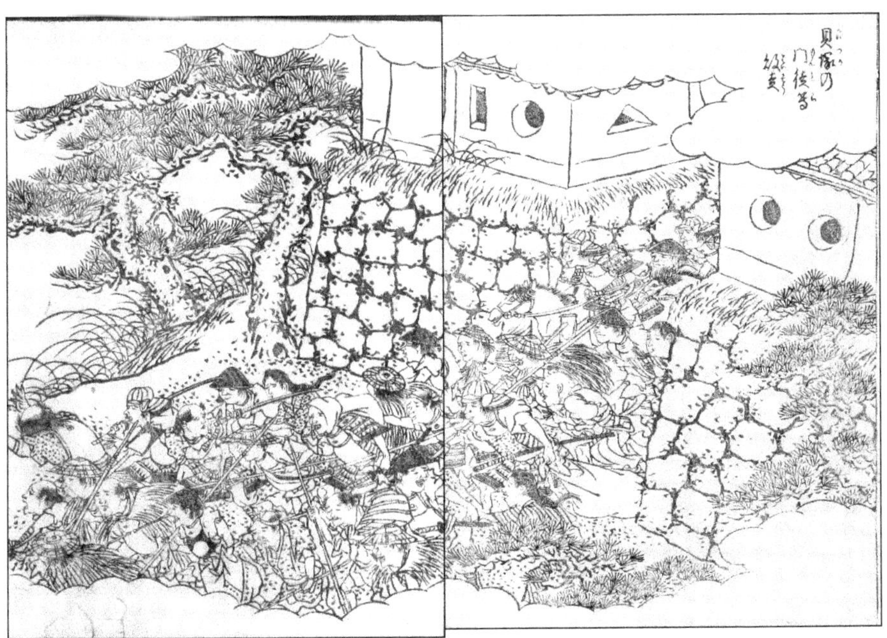

When the Ishiyama War passed into its final years the campaigns became more fragmented as Nobunaga's armies moved against localised armed support This picture shows the fort of Kaizuka in Izumi province. When Nobunaga was about to attack the place in March 1577 the garrison hurriedly fled during the night. Nobunaga went on to assault Suzuki Shigehide's own headquarters at Saika in Kii province (ESSK 2,2).

Supporters of the Honganji from Settsu and Kawachi go to war

Just like the Kaizuka confederacy, other localised groups of Ikkō-ikki joined in the fight against Nobunaga along with their co-religionists in the Osaka forts. Here rural *monto* from Settsu and Kawachi provinces attack some of Nobunaga's troops using improvised weapons including rice-flails and buckets of water (EIKG 3,4).

81

Shimotsuma Raishō uses nobushi tactics against Araki Murashige

Ikkō-ikki raids like the above were perfect examples of the guerrilla warfare campaigns conducted against Nobunaga's isolated armies. Here Shimotsuma Raishō uses *nobushi* tactics against Araki Murashige (1535-86) *Nobushi* means skirmishing by light troops. (EIKG 3,4).

82

Suzuki Shigehide converses with his fellow monto at Ishiyama Honganji

Faced with Nobunaga's persistence and his notable successes against their allies within the coalition, a conference of the Ikkō-ikki was held at the Ishiyama Honganji to determine what their future course of action should be (ESSK 2,7).

83

Nobunaga attacks the walls of the Ishiyama Honganji but is repelled

Throughout this time Nobunaga kept up the pressure on his enemies. A victory at the Second Battle of Kizugawaguchi (not shown here) when he defeated the Mōri navy and disrupted its supply chain, isolated the Ishiyama Honganji still further. Here is a late act of defiance from the Ishiyama Honganji. The defenders are dropping rocks on Nobunaga's troops as they attempt to scale the walls of a fort (ESSK 2,7).

84

As Nobunaga attacks the Honganji the ikki ring the temple bell

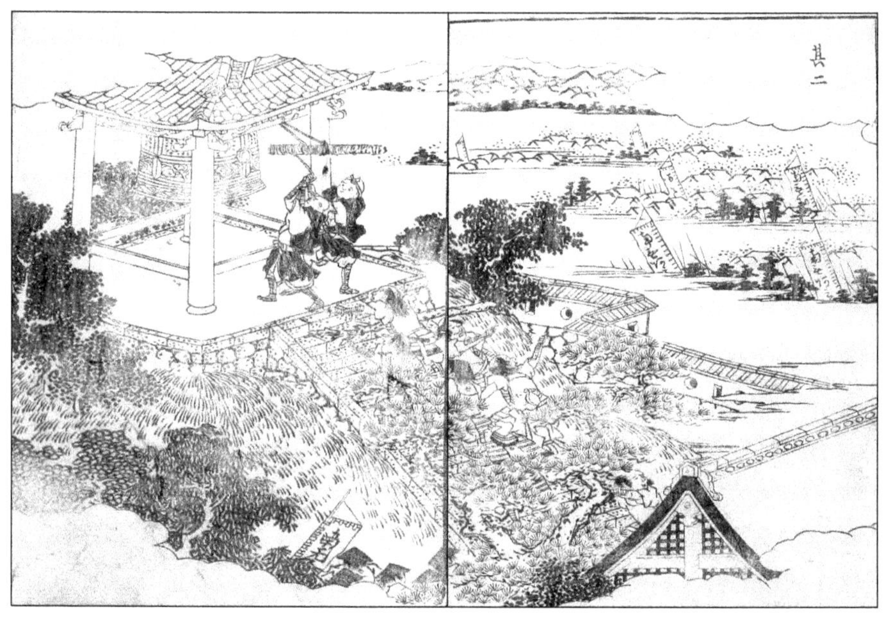

When Nobunaga attacks Ishiyama Honganji the priests of the Ikkō-ikki ring the temple bell to summon assistance, and troops from the outlying forces are soon on the move (ESSK 2,7).

85

Men and women of the Ikkō-ikki advance to the aid of the Honganji

Supporters of the Ikkō-ikki are seen here responding *en masse* to the call to arms. Note the home-made *nenbutsu* banners made by the villagers from straw matting, some of which have the words of the *nenbutsu* written on them in the simple *hiragana* script (ESSK 2,7).

86

Nobunaga makes his final attacks on the Ishiyama Honganji complex

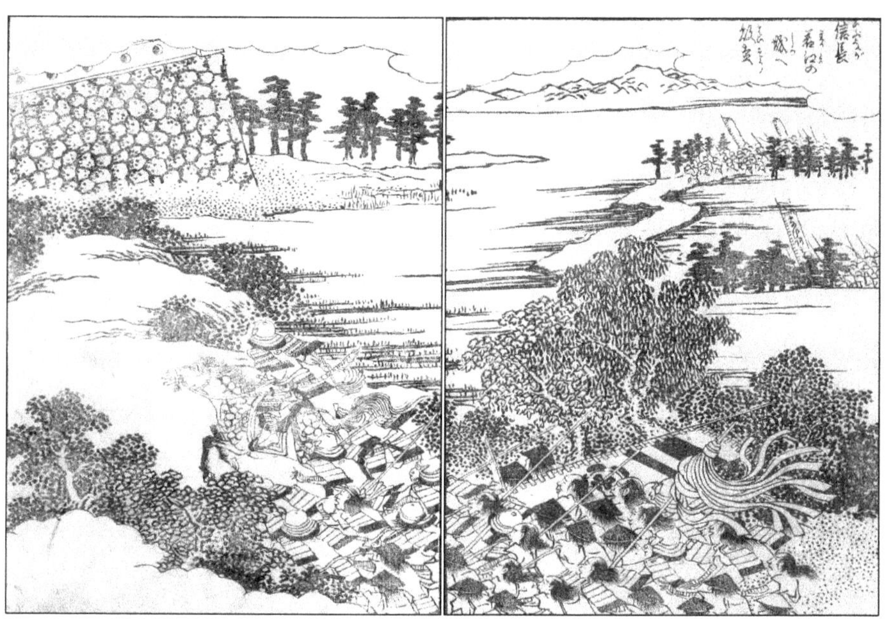

Peace negotiations continued between Nobunaga and Kennyo, but the latter's defiant son Kyōnyo (1558-1614) opposed any settlement with the tyrant and thus became by default the leader of the anti-withdrawal faction in the Honganji. In this picture, in one of his final attacks on the Ishiyama Honganji complex, Nobunaga leads an assault against the walls of a fort and enrages Kyōnyo still further (ESSK 2,7).

87

Civilians flee from Ishiyama Honganji ahead of its surrender

A negotiated surrender mediated by the emperor finally brought the Ishiyama War to an end. In accordance with the peace agreement, Kennyo left Osaka on 22 May 1580 and moved to Saginomori in the Saika area of Kii province where he set up a new Honganji. Fearing retribution from Nobunaga when his armies took over, people of the Ishiyama Honganji fled in terror (ESSK 2,8).

88

The Ishiyama Honganji burns down

Kyōnyo continued to urge defiance against Nobunaga and appealed to the *monto* to rise up once again, but his father Kennyo would not listen and named his younger son Junnyo as his heir instead of Kyōnyo. Nobunaga accordingly increased his blockade of Ishiyama Honganji, and on 10 September 1580 Kyōnyo finally opened the gates of his fortress cathedral. When Nobunaga took possession of it Kyōnyo's supporters set fire to the place and the abandoned Ishiyama Honganji was burned to ashes. It was never rebuilt and is now the site of Osaka Castle (ESSK 2,8).

89

A bad omen is experienced at Saginomori

Certain historical sources add to the *Shinchō-Kō ki* account the events recorded in the following pictures, whereby Nobunaga sent his armies against the Saginomori Honganji in 1582 with orders to kill Kennyo and Kyōnyo Here the troops who are about to attack Saginomori under Niwa Nagahide (1535-85) fear a bad omen when an ikki flag is blown towards them by the wind (EIKG 3,6).

90

The awful news of Nobunaga's death is brought to Saginomori

The bad omen came true when the awful news of Nobunaga's death was brought to the siege lines around Saginomori. His once loyal general Akechi Mitsuhide had carried out a dramatic coup, cornering Nobunaga at the Honnōji in Kyoto and forcing him to commit suicide after a fierce and treacherous attack. In this picture Niwa Nagahide raises the siege immediately and gallops away (ETKK 5,9).

91

Suzuki Shigehide dances for joy at the news of Nobunaga's death

There is a very different reaction to the news inside Saginomori! Instead of being shocked Suzuki Shigehide dances for joy in front of Kennyo when the besieging army departs and the reason for their sudden withdrawal sinks home. Their great enemy Oda Nobunaga is dead (ESSK 2, 9).

92

The warrior monk Komizucha of Negoroji

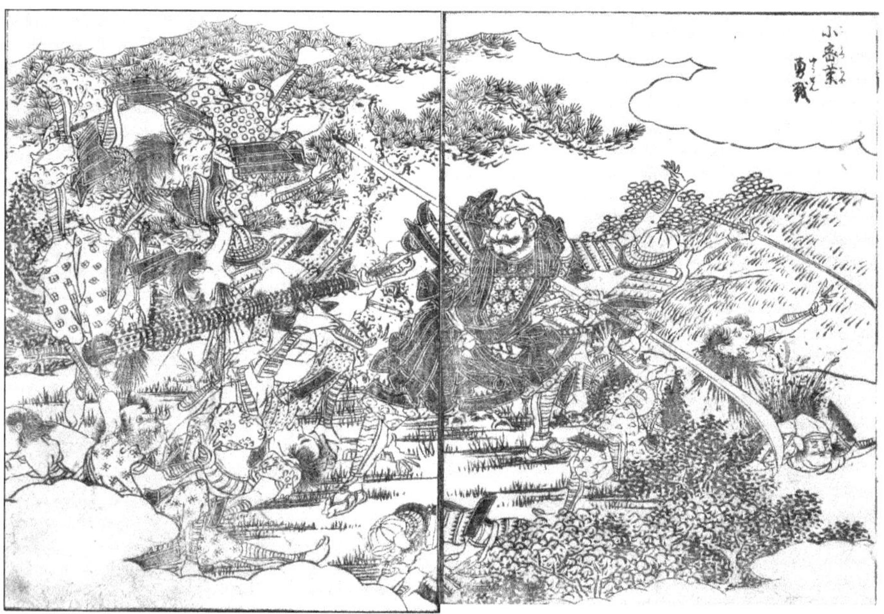

Following the death of Nobunaga Toyotomi Hideyoshi assumed power, vanquishing Akechi Mitsuhide at the battle of Yamazaki in 1582 and routing his fellow generals in a series of rapid and brilliant campaigns in 1583. He eventually met his match in Tokugawa Ieyasu (1542-1616), who courted the support of the Honganji, to whom he promised restoration of their lands in Kaga Ieyasu also sought help against Hideyoshi from the Saika-ikki and the Negoroji warrior monks (ESSK 2,2).

93

Komizucha takes bullets on the blade of his naginata

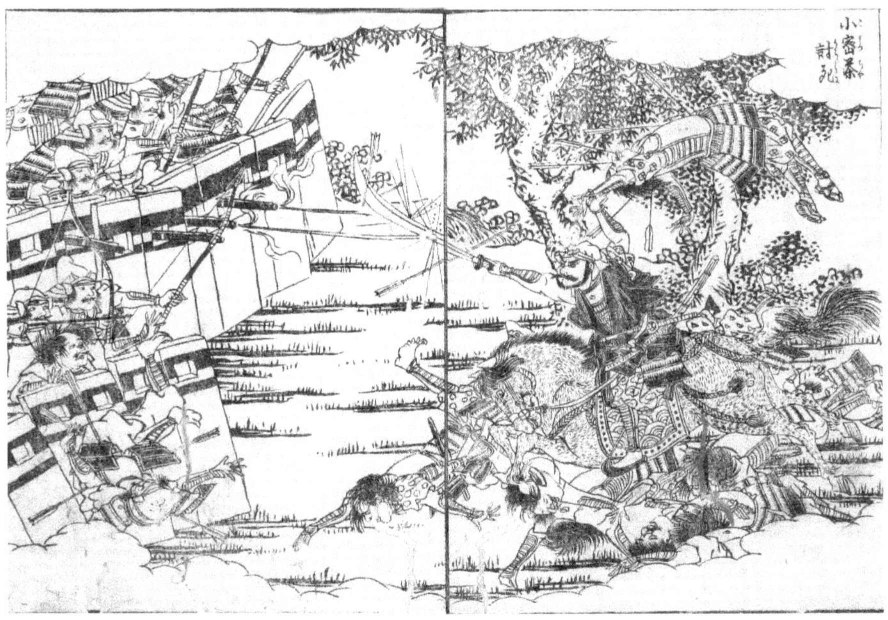

Negoroji and Saika moved against Hideyoshi at the start of the Komaki campaign in 1584. The ultimate result of the operation was a stalemate and a peaceful settlement with Ieyasu, but in 1585 Hideyoshi took his revenger on Negoroji and their allies from Saika. As the classic example of the warrior monk, Komizucha of Negoroji deflects harquebus bullets on his blade of his naginata while lifting an unfortunate victim into the air. In the previous picture he also wields a *bō* (club) (ESSK 2,5).

94

Komizucha is killed by Kimura Matazō

Komizucha is finally overcome and killed by Kimura Matazō, who displays remarkable strength as he slips beneath Komizucha's horse and topples it over (ESSK 2,5).

95

Fierce fighting continues against the warrior monks of Negoroji

Fierce fighting takes place between Hideyoshi's troops and other warrior monks of the Negoroji. The latter are shown shaven-headed and wearing headbands. The surnames of the two samurai grappling with them are identified by their *sashimono* (back flags) as Gotō and Mori (ETTKI 8,3).

96

The Negoroji is burned and destroyed

Hideyoshi settled the fate of the Negoroji by burning down the complex with the monks inside it . Here the monks attempt to flee and salvage their holy treasures (ETK 5,6).

97

The Saika-ikki attack Hideyoshi's rearguard

With Negoroji no more, Hideyoshi turned his attentions to the Saika-ikki and their stronghold of Ōta castle. As adherents of the Honganji, this would be the last time that the *nenbutsu* flags of Ikkō sympathisers would be seen on a battlefield (ESSK 2,10).

98

Hideyoshi floods the Saika-ikki's Ōta castle

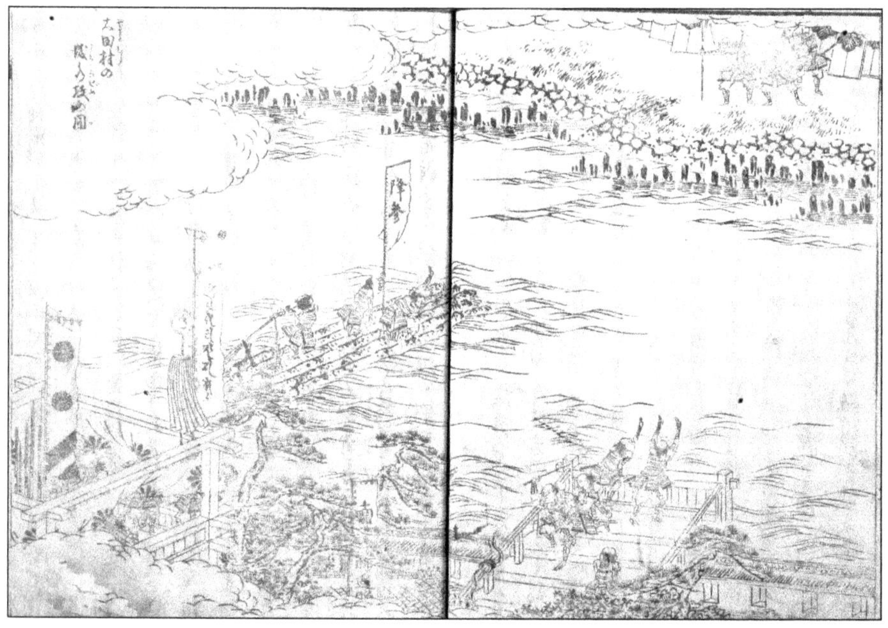

Whereas fire succeeded at Negoroji, water became the decisive weapon at Ōta Castle, because Hideyoshi built a dyke and the castle was flooded. In the foreground we see how it has become a refuge for snakes and weasels as the garrison paddle their way across with a flag of surrender. When Hideyoshi took over Ōta he ordered all those from samurai families to be killed, while farmers were simply disarmed of all weapons and sent back to their lords' fields (ETK 5,6).

99

A conference is held among the Honganji leaders

The pacification of the Saika-ikki meant that Buddhism no longer posed an immediate military threat to Hideyoshi, so he generously allowed the Mount Hiei temples to be rebuilt. The Honganji sect still had the potential to cause future problems, so Hideyoshi took steps to control its development. Junnyo was Kennyo's chosen heir, and in 1591 Hideyoshi granted him a parcel of land in Kyoto for a replacement Honganji headquarters (FSSK 2,7).

100

Kyōnyo visits Tokugawa Ieyasu at Oyama

Hideyoshi died in 1598, and following the battle of Sekigahara in 1600 Tokugawa Ieyasu took over Japan. As part of his plans for preventing militant Buddhism from gaining ground again Ieyasu recognised Kyōnyo as the rightful successor of Kennyo and granted him some land in Kyoto to build his own temple as an alternative and rival headquarters for the Honganji sect. Note in the picture the Jōdo sect's flag that indicates Ieyasu's own religious sensibilities. Its slogan reads "Renounce this filthy world and attain the Pure Land" (EIKG 3,9).

101

The founding of the Higashi-Honganji

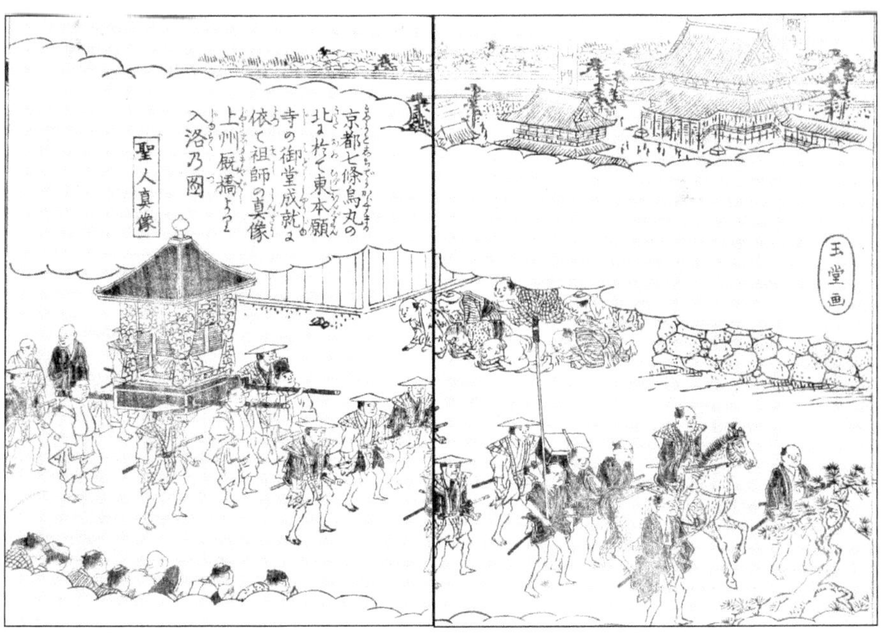

With the founding in 1602 of the Higashi- (Eastern) Honganji in Kyoto a short distance away from the Nishi- (Western) Honganji, the Honganji sect was divided into two, and no more would warriors of the Ikkō-ikki defy the rulers of Japan. The following year Ieyasu would be proclaimed shogun. Under the rule of the Tokugawa family Buddhism, like everything else, would be strictly controlled (EIKG 3,10).

MODERN MEMORIALS TO THE IKKŌ-IKKI

The greatest compliment that Toyotomi Hideyoshi would pay to the warriors of the Ikkō-ikki was to choose the site of the Ishiyama Honganji for his magnificent fortress of Osaka Castle. This memorial stone stands within the castle grounds beside an explanatory notice board.

A memorial to the Nagashima Ikkō-ikki may be found within the courtyard of the rebuilt Ganshōji in Nagashima. The site of the original Ganshōji now lies under the sea: testament to the huge changes to the landscape of the Nagashima Delta over the centuries since the Ishiyama War.

The most moving of the Ikkō-ikki memorials is this one at the restored castle of Torigoe in Ishikawa Prefecture. As a commemoration of the Kaga Ikkō-ikki, it lays stark emphasis on the tens of thousands of people executed in cold blood by Nobunaga over a period of many years of warfare.

FURTHER READING

Readers who are interested in learning more about the Ikkō ikki are very fortunate, because three excellent works about the subject are available in English. *Buddhism and the State in Sixteenth-Century Japan* by Neil McMullin (Princeton University Press, 1984) contains a highly detailed account of the events of the Ishiyama War based on contemporary records and letters. *Japonius Tyrannus: The Japanese warlord Oda Nobunaga reconsidered* by Jeroen Lamers (Hotei Press, 2000) is an outstanding modern biography of Nobunaga, in which the author challenges McMullin's views about the centrality of the Honganji's threat to Nobunaga's career.

For a translation of the most important work on which such arguments are based the reader should consult (and will greatly enjoy!) *The Chronicle of Lord Nobunaga by Ōta Gyūichi* translated and edited by J.S.A. Elisonas and J.P Lamers (Brill, 2011). This is a careful yet exciting translation of *Shinchō-Kō ki*, the biography compiled by one of Nobunaga's own retainers who was an eye-witness to many of the events he describes in great detail. To some extent the *Ehon Shūi Shinchō ki* used here is an illustrated version of *Shinchō-Kō ki*.

There are numerous works available in the Japanese language of course, and one recently published volume has made a particularly interesting contribution to the history of the Ikkō-ikki. It is written by Kikumi Enya and is entitled *Ishiyama kassen wo yomi naosu*. (Hōzōkan, 2021). Enya challenges the very concept of a ten year-long Ishiyama War, and shows how the idea of the Ikkō-ikki has been subject to centuries of myth-making, for which the pictorial sources used for the images in this present volume played a vital role.

Finally, for a good idea of what the fortified temples of the Ikkō-ikki actually looked like and how they were defended against Nobunaga, I recommend my own modest publication *Japanese Fortified Temples and Monasteries AD 710-1602* (Osprey 2005).

INDEX TO THE ILLUSTRATIONS

The references which follow are to the picture numbers, not pages

www.ingramcontent.com/pod-product-compliance
Ingram Content Group UK Ltd.
Pitfield, Milton Keynes, MK11 3LW, UK
UKHW022018190726
13853UKWH00005B/2001

9 798796 811474